The Impacts of China's Rise on the Pacific and the World

The Impacts of China's Rise on the Pacific and the World

Wei-Chiao Huang
Huizhong Zhou
Editors

2018

W.E. Upjohn Institute for Employment Research
Kalamazoo, Michigan

Library of Congress Cataloging-in-Publication Data

Names: Huang, Wei-Chiao, editor. | Zhou, Huizhong, 1947- editor.
Title: The impacts of China's rise on the Pacific and the world / Wei-Chiao Huang,
  Huizong Zhou, editors.
Description: Kalamazoo, Mich. : W.E. Upjohn Institute for Employment Research,
  [2018] | Includes index.
Identifiers: LCCN 2017055606 | ISBN 9780880996327 (pbk. : alk. paper) | ISBN
  0880996323 (pbk. : alk. paper) | ISBN 9780880996334 (hardcover : alk. paper) |
  ISBN 0880996331 (hardcover : alk. paper) | ISBN 9780880996358 (ebook) | ISBN
  0880996358 (ebook)
Subjects: LCSH: China—economic conditions. | China—foreign economic relations.
Classification: LCC HC427.95 .I47 2018 | DDC 330.951—dc23 LC record available
  at https://lccn.loc.gov/2017055606

The facts presented in this study and the observations and viewpoints expressed are
the sole responsibility of the authors. They do not necessarily represent positions of
the W.E. Upjohn Institute for Employment Research.

Cover design by Carol A.S. Derks.
Index prepared by Diane Worden.
Printed in the United States of America.
Printed on recycled paper.

Contents

Acknowledgments   vii

1   **Introduction**   1
    Wei-Chiao Huang and Huizhong Zhou

2   **The United States and the China Challenge**   15
    Murray Scot Tanner

3   **Is There a Xi Jinping Model of Economic Reform?**   27
    Barry Naughton

4   **Understanding the Major Threats to China's Economic Growth**   43
    Wing Thye Woo

5   **State Enterprise Reform in China: Grasp or Release?**   83
    Mary E. Lovely and Yang Liang

6   **Why Exit Rights Are the Key to the Reduction of Urban-Rural Income Disparity in China**   107
    Guanzhong James Wen

7   **Trade, Migration, and Growth: Evidence from China**   123
    Xiaodong Zhu

Authors   139

Index   141

About the Institute   155

Acknowledgments

The chapters in this volume are based on lectures from the fifty-second Werner Sichel Lecture Series in 2015–2016. The editors gratefully appreciate financial support from the Western Michigan University Department of Economics, the College of Arts and Sciences, and the Timothy Light Center for Chinese Studies; and the W.E. Upjohn Institute for Employment Research. We are also grateful to the editorial production staff at the Upjohn Institute, particularly Allison Hewitt Colosky, for the superb editorial services rendered in the publication of this volume. Finally, we are grateful for the cooperation and insightful analysis provided by the six esteemed speakers of the series and chapter authors.

1
Introduction

Wei-Chiao Huang
Huizhong Zhou
Western Michigan University

After three decades of rapid economic growth, China has become the second-largest economy in the world. Its rise has driven its search for resources, opportunities, and outside influences, and economic expansion will inevitably be followed by political influences and potentially overbearing military strength. In just four years, 2014–2017, China's outward investment and construction combined exceeded $800 billion. China has also established the Asian Infrastructure Investment Bank, which rivals the World Bank and the Asian Development Bank. Its economic expansion has inevitably brought about conflicts with its neighboring countries, including South Korea, Japan, and Vietnam, and it has recently shifted from being conciliatory to being more assertive toward territorial disputes. The ripples created by China's first aircraft carrier are bound to travel across the Pacific and reach the shoreline of the United States. One of the contributors to this volume, Murray Scot Tanner, quotes former Deputy Assistant Secretary of State Dr. Tom Christensen: "China's return to great power status is perhaps the most important challenge in twenty-first century American diplomacy" (Christensen 2015, p. 1). This assessment of the relationship between the two nations has been epitomized by recent events that have occupied the center stage of the U.S. trade and foreign policy, including tensions in the South China Sea and diplomacy toward North Korea and its nuclear and missile activity.

With this background, the 2015–2016 Werner Sichel Lecture Series featured six prominent experts who shared their insights on China and U.S.-China relations. Their lectures help put in perspective China's rise and its impact on the Pacific region, and the relationship and potential conflicts between the United States and China. This collection presents the edited version of their lectures.

In Chapter 2, Tanner explores five underlying factors in the U.S.-China relationship that pose challenges for the United States: 1) China's rapidly expanding national interests and its increasing power to assert and protect them, 2) China's governance problems and their lack of commitment to cooperation, 3) China's view of security and the complexity of building U.S.-Chinese "strategic trust," 4) mobilizing the United States' allies and partners, and 5) the challenge at home.

China's leadership remains committed to an established set of long-standing, key security interests—most notably its core interests of protecting Chinese Communist Party rule, maintenance of social stability, sustained economic and technological growth, and protection of China's national unity, sovereignty, and territorial integrity. The frontlines of these existing interests, however, are expanding beyond East Asia and to extended arenas of national security. These include maintaining energy security, protecting its expanding overseas investments and the millions of expatriate Chinese workers in unstable environments abroad, asserting and protecting its expanding maritime security interests, advancing and protecting its communications security and military security interests in the space and cyber realms, and helping to secure a stable global environment conducive to the country's sustained development. China's expanding interests inevitably define many arenas in which the United States and China share overlapping but not necessarily identical interests. While these overlaps make the U.S.-China relationship increasingly complex and challenging, they also widen the range of issues on which the two countries actively cooperate.

Another challenge that the United States faces in dealing with China is deficiencies of China's bureaucracy in implementing agreements. With China's prominent and extensive presence economically and politically in the world, it needs China's public support to address key international problems. However, even if leading authorities in Beijing nominally support certain international norms and agreements, China's capabilities to enforce, implement, or oversee its commitments often may be inadequate. Tanner points out that Chinese local officials and state companies often "control more than enough resources to undermine some international problem-solving efforts." China's international partners, including the United States, must work with Beijing to urge it to develop and strengthen its governance institutions and policy-implementing capacities, and get China to demonstrate sustained resolve in actively supporting and enforcing a wide array of international solutions.

The third challenge is so-called strategic trust between the United States and China. For many years, the Chinese have often told their U.S. partners that our two great powers need to overcome strategic mistrust or build strategic trust. However, according to Tanner, this call has typically "been accompanied by lists of actions that the United States should take that demonstrate respect for China's core national security interests." These actions relate to reevaluating the U.S.-Asian alliance structure, ending U.S. reconnaissance flights near China's territory, decreasing U.S. support to allies and partners locked in tensions with, or lifting restrictions on U.S. technology sales to, China.

The fourth challenge relates to China's role in the South China Sea and U.S. relations with allies in that region. The United States will have to strike a balance among three missions: 1) signaling a joint resolve between the United States and its allies to protect our common interests in response to Beijing's assertive behavior; 2) attempting to reassure Beijing that our continued alliance and partnership with Asian-Pacific nations are not aimed at undermining or encircling China; and 3) continuing to search for new areas where the United States and its allies can enhance nontraditional security cooperation with China in the region, such as counterpiracy, antiterrorism, and humanitarian assistance and disaster relief.

Finally, Tanner identifies a challenge here at home. To modify a continual long-term policy toward a rising China, it will require "more focused U.S. attention to China in our mass media, classrooms, and elsewhere. Discussions need go beyond an oversimplified debate over China as partner or China as adversary." A good understanding of China and its relationship with the United States by the public is required for a stable long-term approach to budgetary politics that supports the policies toward China. According to Tanner, U.S. politics at home in turn has a major impact on our capacity to engage, cooperate with, and compete with China, and work with our allies and partners to promote and protect our interests in the region.

China's foreign relations have become more assertive in recent years, and its domestic politics has undergone drastic changes. The change in position on foreign affairs is perhaps a result of changes in China's domestic politics. Since Xi Jinping assumed leadership in

2012, he has launched a series of political maneuvers to crack down on corruption, amass his own political power, and suppress freedom of speech. In addition to the overhaul of the bureaucratic machine, Xi appears to have a different vision of the economy as well, which relies more on governments than markets. In Chapter 3, Barry Naughton gives a timely assessment of the prospects of the Chinese economy under its newly established leader.

Xi Jinping laid out an ambitious program of reform in the Third Plenum Resolution of November 2013. However, since that time, progress on economic reform has been slow and uneven. Naughton, relying on his insightful understanding of the economy, explains why Xi's model may fail. His arguments follow three closely related steps. First, the period of "miracle growth" in China ends; second, Xi Jinping's policy agenda generally relies on a strengthening of government and, especially, party intervention in the society and economy; and third, as a result, Xi's policy regime is marked by and mired in inconsistent and sometimes contradictory objectives.

The Chinese economy grew at an average rate of just over 10 percent a year between 1978 and 2010. However, in 2010 the growth rate fell below 8 percent and in 2016 it was around 6.7 percent. As China moves into middle-income range it faces fundamental challenges. "Cheap China" is not cheap any longer. Wages for unskilled workers have risen rapidly, particularly between 2008 and 2013. Producers of garments, shoes, and sporting goods are beginning to move their businesses to Vietnam and Bangladesh, where wages are lower than in China. This change in labor costs strongly correlates with the end of the miracle growth era in earlier developing economies such as Japan, Korea, and Taiwan. However, the "one-child policy" has exacerbated the labor cost increase in China.

Another challenge is the debt overhang that China has built up over the past seven to eight years. China has been aggressively expanding bank lending to cope with the global financial crisis and maintain high rate of growth. For example, the debt accumulated by local government jumped from 17 to 35 percent of GDP between 2007 and 2014. Naughton says that "while the overall debt level is not yet unsustainable, the trajectory certainly is. China needs to find a way both to slow the increase in debt and to restructure the portion of debt that will never be repaid."

In the face of such economic challenges, Xi Jinping's administration adopted an approach that relied more on government intervention than markets. As an economy approached the world technological frontier, it became less likely that bureaucrats had an advantage over private actors in predicting technological or sectoral evolution. Both Japan and Korea had successfully followed this approach. Naughton writes, "Although China has a very different political and economic system from Japan and Korea, the general direction in which China has evolved since 1978 seemed consistent with the earlier evolution of Korea and Japan. Since the 1980s, the Chinese government has stepped back from many aspects of society, and as China became richer, Chinese society became more diverse and tolerant. However, to a remarkable extent, Xi has sought to reverse this direction. He has consolidated his own individual power more rapidly than anyone expected, and he has established his own personal dominance of the political process more thoroughly than most believed possible." In particular, he took over a new "leadership small group" (LSG), which had direct authority over the economic reform process. This group represented a significant departure from past Chinese practice, by which economic policy was run directly out of the State Council by the premier. Xi's direct control of economic policy meant that the success or failure of economic reforms in China today would be a reflection on the validity of the "Xi Jinping model." Naughton then examines three major reform initiatives during 2015: restructuring local government debt, opening the stock market, and reforming state enterprise.

Beginning in 2014, the minister of finance laid out an ambitious program of local debt restructuring. The plan was to cap debt at the 2014 level and then begin to transform debt into new, local government "municipal bonds." However, this initial program of debt restructuring failed. Buyers and sellers were unable to agree on an interest rate. The government was forced to withdraw the offer.

Chinese policymakers also laid out an ambitious reform of equity markets. The Chinese stock markets are highly "political"; that is, stock prices swing with intended, perceived, or rumored changes in policies. Anxious to revitalize the markets, some policymakers and government media zealously promoted a rosy picture of the markets. The entire political leadership, including Xi Jinping, had been complicit in statements that directly or indirectly encouraged the stock market bubble. As a result, the Shanghai Stock Exchange Index soared in June and then crashed in July, leaving China's leaders anxious. After the plummet, Premier Li Keqiang presided over a series of meetings designed to bail out the stock market. The China Securities Finance Corporation was provided with unlimited liquidity to buy up "red chip" stocks. After the bailout, new listings were once again suspended. Interest by overseas investors quickly evaporated. Not only was the market still in a bear mode, but the added risk of unpredictable government policy was too great for most foreign investors to take.

Attempts to further reform state-owned enterprises (SOEs) did not fare well either. The Resolution of the Third Plenum (November 2013) introduced several innovative approaches, such as an expanded role for "mixed ownership," new investment funds that would manage government wealth, and a role for employee share owning. The efforts to turn these ideas into reality quickly froze. Then, as Naughton explains, "in the summer of 2014, the Reform LSG made several decisions that thoroughly upended the stalled SOE reform process. Most strikingly, the LSG approved a limitation on the salaries of SOE managers, which was designed to bring SOE managers' salaries in line with those of bureaucrats at a similar level. The abrupt adoption of these salary caps underlined the extent to which Xi Jinping was seeking to achieve mixed objectives in his approach to state-owned enterprises." Another case of confusion of policies and setback of SOE reforms was a decision to set up a new specialized "SOE Reform LSG," which gave the economic bureaucracy more control over SOEs.

Naughton summarizes that by the end of 2015, all three of these reform initiatives of the Plenum had failed. He further points out that "there may be a deeper contradiction between the requirements of this stage of economic reform and the exercise of authority by a single individual. An authoritative leader may be helpful in the first stage of reform, adapting to crises and throwing off old constraints. However, at a certain point, market-oriented reforms require that leader to step back and allow market forces to work without constraint." China today has developed into a satisfactorily functioning market economy. It needs at this stage independent regulatory and financial institutions, which have not been a prominent part of the Xi Jinping reform package. The year 2015 thus "provides little support for the idea that an authoritative Xi

Jinping leadership can contribute effectively to the economic reform process."

In Chapter 4, Wing Thye Woo notes that China has been experiencing or may encounter in the near future three classes of failures that will interrupt the miraculous growth that China has achieved in the past 30 years: 1) a hardware failure from the breakdown of an economic mechanism, 2) a software failure from flaws in governance that create frequent widespread social disorders, and 3) a power supply failure from hitting either a natural or an externally imposed limit. He then elaborates and illustrates these failures by citing important cases and factors.

Of the hardware failure, Woo stresses state banks' solvency and the central government's fiscal health. The state-owned banks (SOBs) had in the past accumulated enormous bad debts to the point of insolvency. The central government previously had rescued the banks by injecting new capital. If the state is perceived to be able and willing to bail out the SOBs, depositors would retain their confidence in the banks regardless of the actual state of their balance sheets. The important question is, how many more rounds of bank recapitalization can China afford without generating a fiscal crisis? Woo claims that the government can hardly afford to recapitalize the SOBs without upsetting confidence in the financial markets about the soundness of China's fiscal regime. The task then is to stop losses in the SOBs in order to ensure fiscal sustainability. The solution lies in imposing a hard budget constraint on the SOBs.

Woo suggests that the operations of SOBs could be improved by bringing in foreign strategic investors who would be part of the management team, and by removing the influence of the local governments on bank operations. He writes, "Another way to harden the budget constraint faced by the SOBs is to privatize some of their branches and use the performance of the new private banks to gauge the performance of the remaining SOBs. The privatization of some branches will also help convince the SOB managers that the government is indeed determined not to recapitalize SOBs in the future."

Citing two cases, Woo deems government corruption and dereliction as major factors of software failures. In one, the former director of China's Food and Drug Safety Agency took bribes from pharmaceutical and food companies in exchange for approvals of drugs and production licenses. The market was flooded with counterfeit products and tainted and substandard food and drugs, and tens of thousands of people were sickened or killed every year as a result. The other case pertains to government failure to protect workers. Child labor and slaves were not uncommon in rural and remote regions, especially in the mining businesses.

For power supply failures, Woo's main concerns are trade conflicts and environmental disasters. China's chronic and growing overall trade surplus reveals a serious problem in China's economy—its dysfunctional financial system. The banking system favors SOEs to the extent that the returns of investment have been extremely low and eventually created huge excess capacity. High ratios of nonperform loans in the state banks and excess capacity have triggered a slowdown in bank loans. This cutback has created an excess of savings because the SOB-dominated financial sector does not rechannel the released savings to finance the investment of the private sector. Woo suggests that the optimum solution to the problem of excess saving is not for the government to absorb it by increasing its budget deficit, but to establish an improved mechanism for coordinating private savings and private investments.

While the nonstate sector has risen tremendously in China throughout the reform process, the state-owned and state-controlled enterprises have remained an important aspect of the Chinese economy. In fact, despite three decades of aggressive enterprise reforms involving privatization of some state firms and retaining/restructuring of others, the remaining state enterprises continue to dominate some major sectors of the Chinese economy and have also emerged as global titans. In Chapter 5, Mary E. Lovely and Yang Liang address the issue of state enterprise reform that Naughton touches on in Chapter 3. They examine the characteristics of firms that were retained by the Chinese state and those that were released to the private sector between 1998 and 2006. Their empirical analysis is conducted using microdata from China's National Bureau of Statistics, specifically, China's Annual Survey of Industrial Production.

Lovely and Liang begin their analysis by tracking the evolution of enterprises away from China's state sector over time. They first describe the inherent difficulties encountered by researchers to identify the state-owned and state-controlled firms. The difficulties stem from various definitions of state control, limited data, and opaque ownership arrangements. They then explain their approach to defining a firm as state owned and state controlled when it is registered as an SOE, when the share of registered capital held directly by the state exceeds or equals 50 percent, or when the state is reported as the controlling shareholder. Using this classification, they contribute to the literature by providing new estimates of the size of the state sector. Specifically, they find that about 5 percent of total enterprises were state owned and controlled in 2006, and that these enterprises supply more than 30 percent of industrial output.

Lovely and Liang's major contribution to the literature, which also constitutes the main part of this chapter, is the insight gained from their econometric analysis examining the characteristics of those enterprises chosen by the state to be released and which it chose to grasp. Based on the various perspectives in the literature on how the state chose which assets to grasp and which to release to private owners, they formed hypotheses about the relationship between initial firm characteristics and the likelihood that they remained state controlled. They test these hypotheses using a linear probability model for two time periods, 1998–2002 and 2002–2006. Their main findings are that in both periods, firms that were larger and more viable financially, but had lower revenues relative to assets, were more likely to be retained by the state. Firms with low labor productivity, an indication of legacy burdens, were also more likely to be retained. Additionally, after 2002, firms affiliated with higher levels of governments were much less likely to be privatized.

After presenting their regression results, Lovely and Liang review recent assessments made by several groups of researchers on the performance and productivity gaps between the state and nonstate sectors. They summarize the findings of recent analyses of the success of the restructured state enterprises in reducing factor misallocations and, hence, in contributing to productivity growth. Considering their estimates, the lower productivity of state-controlled firms appears to be a natural consequence of how enterprises were grasped and released. Therefore, it is not surprising that average state sector productivity continued to lag behind the private sector, despite innovation in the form of state control. Finally, they use their analysis of the grasp-or-release decision to highlight some of the challenges of continued SOE reforms in the future.

In Chapter 6, Guanzhong James Wen advocates for a significant reform in the land tenure system in China. Despite the phenomenal growth of China's economy, which is an unprecedented achievement and probably cannot be surpassed by other nations, its income disparity has become the worst in East Asia. In particular, its urban/rural income ratio has become one of—if not the—worst in the world. Unlike the experience of China since 1979, developed economies and more recently East Asian economies, such as South Korea and Taiwan, have been able to achieve growth without suffering from substantially worsening rural/urban disparity. Why can they achieve that? According to Wen, it is because the farmers in those economies were allowed to freely trade their land, and freely migrate to and settle in urban areas.

Why can't China also achieve that? Wen explains that China's rural population is constrained by two institutional barriers depriving them to legally share urban prosperity and to accumulate wealth on equal footing: the hukou system and the land tenure system. China's hukou system has made urbanization almost exclusively inaccessible to the rural population, turning urbanization into urbanizing mainly land instead of rural population. The hukou (family registration) system was officially promulgated in 1958 by the Chinese government to control the movement of people between urban and rural areas. Individuals were broadly categorized as a rural or urban worker. A worker seeking to move from the country to urban areas to take up nonagricultural work would have to apply through the relevant bureaucracies. The number of workers allowed to make such moves was tightly controlled. Migrant workers still need to obtain several passes to work in provinces other than their own. People who work outside their authorized domain or geographical area do not qualify for employer-provided housing, health care, or other urban amenities. Even their children are not eligible to attend municipal schools where their parents are working since they don't have urban hukou. As a result, there are an estimated 60 million children left behind in rural areas, separated from their parents working in urban areas. The poor educational condition in rural areas dictates that most of them will have limited human capital and will acquire low social mobility and low income in the future. This vicious cycle dampens the prospect for China to improve its urban-rural income distribution, even though the central government is now moving to gradually dismantle the hukou system. Big cities are given some autonomy to decide on their own hukou policy, and the towns and small cities are also urged to open up to rural migration. Only time will tell how effective and how soon China can ultimately eliminate control over free migration and free settlement.

According to Wen, the prevailing land tenure system is an even bigger barrier than the hukou system, as it provides "local governments either a legal basis or an excuse to take rural land for urban development. Under this system the government becomes a monopsony in buying farmers' land and a monopoly in auctioning off the leaseholds to developers." The land price is thus seriously distorted, either inflated or suppressed. Wen articulates the impossibility of developing a true land market under the current constitution, particularly Article 10, which stipulates that land in the cities is owned by the state and land in the rural and suburban areas is owned by collectives. Rural collectives are not allowed to trade land among themselves, let alone the individual farmers. Even if a collective is inefficient or corrupt, or its leaders are abusive, members cannot exit with their share of land to regroup a new collective on a truly voluntary basis. Wen points out that in the absence of a truly functioning land market, inefficiencies and distortions abound, manifested by the contrasts of "on one side, ghost towns, idling apartment buildings, and deserted industrial parks are emerging everywhere, especially in China's vast inland, but in its coastal areas, housing prices are skyrocketing; on the other side, most of the 2.6 hundred million migrant workers are living in shelters, slums, ghettos, or urban villages, which are being bulldozed by the local governments, aggravating the shortage of affordable housing."

Wen concludes his chapter with a proposal of how to reform the land tenure system in China. The key, he says, is that farmers should be given the exit rights from the compulsory collective land ownership and that land trading should be legalized as long as the land use (zoning) is not changed. Wen also advocates that China should abolish its Hukou system as soon as possible. He expects that with these two reforms implemented, China can accelerate the absorption of rural surplus labor and significantly improve its urban-rural income disparity.

In Chapter 7, Xiaodong Zhu provides convincing evidence of the benefits of reducing restrictions on movements of goods and people in an economy, using China's experience between 2000 and 2005 as a case study. This chapter corroborates with Chapter 6, as Zhu's findings provide quantitative endorsement of Wen's proposal to lift restrictions and facilitate rural to urban migration by granting farmers exit rights from compulsory collective land ownership and dismantling the Hukou system.

Zhu begins by discussing the state of the Chinese economy in year 2000 and then motivates the study by describing some important changes that happened between 2000 and 2005, particularly those that reduced migration and trade costs. Next, Zhu reports findings from a previous working paper (Tombe and Zhu 2015) on the extent of migration and trade cost reductions. Specifically, Tombe and Zhu find that overall, migration costs declined to 84 percent of their initial level, and that costs to switch provinces fell the most, from 32.6 to 19.8 percent. They find that trade costs within China declined by 11 percent, and trade costs between China and the world on average declined by 8 percent. Also, China's costs of importing from the rest of the world declined more than China's costs of exporting to the rest of the world.

Zhu then reports the quantitative impacts of these changes in migration and trade costs on aggregate productivity and welfare. Specifically, because of lower internal trade costs, aggregate welfare increased significantly, by nearly 11 percent, whereas external trade cost reductions resulted in a smaller gain of only 3.1 percent. Further, the reductions of migration costs (mostly due to relaxation of the stringent Hukou system restrictions) increased the number of interprovincial migrants by more than 80 percent. Increased migration flows were also beneficial for China as a whole; real GDP and welfare rose by 4.8 percent and 8.5 percent, respectively. Lastly, Zhu highlights the results from their growth decomposition exercise that decomposed China's overall growth between 2000 and 2005 into four components: 1) productivity growth, 2) lower internal trade costs, 3) lower international trade costs, and 4) lower internal migration costs. Overall, reductions in trade and migration frictions together accounted for about one-third of China's aggregate growth. Specifically, reductions in internal and migration costs contributed roughly one quarter of growth, whereas international trade cost reductions accounted for only 7 percent of the overall growth. This finding challenges the conventional wisdom that the main reason for China's rapid growth is external trade liberalization associated with China's entry in the WTO. Tombe and Zhu's (2015) study shows that, at least for the period from 2000 to 2005, internal policy reforms undertaken by the Chinese government that lowered internal trade and migration costs contributed more to China's growth than external trade cost reductions (27 percent versus 7 percent). Thus, Professor Zhu concludes that if China continues to pursue reforms to dismantle the Hukou system and further internal liberalizations, we can expect increases in China's aggregate GDP and welfare to continue in the future.

China has been rising rapidly since the late 1970s, when it launched market-oriented reforms and opened gradually to the world economy. Thirty years later, in 2010, China surpassed Japan in GDP and became the second-largest economy of the world. The attainment of this status was regarded as a milestone of the reform movement; it has since been referred to as the reforms of 30 years. The editors of this volume published a collection in 2012, titled *Dragon versus Eagle: The Chinese Economy and U.S.-China Relations* (Huang and Zhou 2012), which summarizes and evaluates the achievements and problems of the 30 years. Now the reform is quickly nearing its 40 years. Can we call it a reform of 40 years, implying that it follows the same direction and spirit of the previous 30 years? The term has not appeared yet, perhaps for a good reason. Recent policies and measures appear to have deviated from the previous path, especially since 2013, when Xi Jinping assumed leadership. In the name of anticorruption, Xi has not only concentrated power in his own hand within the Party but also tightened control over society by cracking down on freedom of speech. The leadership has shown distrust toward the private economy and markets. Private enterprises are required to set up Party branches, and financial markets asked to "place politics ahead of profits." Now that the twice-a-decade Party Congress has ended and Xi Jinping further consolidated his power, the economic and political changes that were cultivated in the past five years will take a more definite direction and shape. The Party documents declared it was a beginning of a new era. While the Chinese populace at large acclimates and becomes desensitized to the rhetoric, scholars, policymakers, and businessmen, in China and abroad, are anxiously watching what these changes will lead to and how they may impact the Chinese economy. The China experts in this collection have touched on some of the concerns and shared their insights on possible consequences. We believe that this volume will provide a backdrop for anticipating and understanding developments and changes in China in the near future.

References

Christensen, Thomas J. 2015. *The China Challenge: Shaping the Choices of a Rising Power.* New York: W.W. Norton.

Huang, Wei-Chiao, and Huizhong Zhou, eds. 2012. *Dragon versus Eagle: The Chinese Economy and U.S.-China Relations.* Kalamazoo, MI: W.E. Upjohn Institute for Employment Research.

Tombe, Trevor, and Xiaodong Zhu. 2015. "Trade, Migration and Productivity: A Quantitative Analysis of China." Department of Economics Working Paper No. 542. Toronto, Ontario: University of Toronto.

2

The United States and the China Challenge

Murray Scot Tanner
CNA Corporation

It is hard to dispute the judgment of Princeton scholar and former Deputy Assistant Secretary of State Dr. Tom Christensen that "China's return to great power status is perhaps the most important challenge in twenty-first century American diplomacy" (Christensen 2015, p. 1). Because of China's decades of rapid economic growth, and its investment of that growth in expanding its diplomatic and military power, there are now very few issues in U.S. diplomacy in which China does not play a major role. During meetings between Chinese Communist Party General Secretary Xi Jinping and President Obama, notably their 2015 Washington Summit and their 2016 meeting during the Nuclear Security Summit, the two leaders have wrestled with important issues of cooperation—such as climate change and responding to North Korea's nuclear weapons and missile tests—while confronting equally important issues of competition and confrontation—such as territorial disputes in the South China Sea and threats to cyber security (Tanner 2016).

This chapter explores five underlying factors in the U.S.-China relationship that pose particularly strong challenges for the United States:

1) China's rapidly expanding national interests and its increasing power to assert and protect them,

2) China's governance problems and their challenge to cooperation,

3) China's thinking about security and the challenge of building U.S.-Chinese "strategic trust,"

4) the challenge of mobilizing U.S. allies and partners, and

5) the challenge at home.

CHINA'S RAPIDLY EXPANDING NATIONAL INTERESTS AND BEIJING'S POWER TO ASSERT THEM

Driving the emergence of many new or deepening challenges in U.S.-China relations has been China's expanding national security interests—both within its region and globally—and Beijing's growing capacity to assert or protect them. China's emerging interests result mainly from its three decades of sustained economic growth and expanding economic, diplomatic, and military power. China's leadership, at its core, remains committed to an established set of long-standing, key security interests—most notably protecting Chinese Communist Party rule, maintaining social stability, sustaining economic and technological growth, and protecting China's national unity, sovereignty, and territorial integrity. But the front lines of these existing interests are expanding beyond East Asia, and China has increasingly demonstrated its growing concern over at least six emerging arenas of national security interest (Tanner and Mackenzie 2015):

1) Maintaining energy security, especially access to petroleum and natural gas through the Indian Ocean region and Russia and Central Asia.

2) Protecting China's expanding overseas investments and the millions of expatriate Chinese workers in unstable environments abroad.

3) Asserting and protecting China's expanding maritime security interests—its territorial and resource claims in the South China Sea and East China Sea, and its access to trade, investments, and resources in "distant seas" regions via strategic lines of communication, such as Malacca, the Persian Gulf, the Horn of Africa, and increasingly the Arctic.

4) Protecting China's increasing economic, security, and domestic stability concerns along its west-southwest borderland regions, which are predominantly populated with ethnic and religious minority groups. These interests include China's concerns over long-running waves of Uyghur and Tibetan social discontent, but also China's strategic relations with India, Pakistan, Afghanistan, Iran, and Central Asia, and China's ongo-

ing plan to establish a new "Silk Road" of trade and investment ties.

5) Advancing and protecting its communications security and military security interests in the space and cyber realms.

6) Helping to secure a stable global environment conducive to China's sustained development.

For the past decade, China has been engaged in a major internal discussion of how it conceives and prioritizes these interests, including debates over which interests the country can now afford to assert and protect, something it has never been able to promote in the past. Related are discussions of how to develop and employ new strategies, tactics, and resources to assert and protect these interests—including diplomatic, economic, law enforcement, administrative, cyber/informational, intelligence, and military resources. As one part of this, the People's Liberation Army's (PLA) doctrinal writers have been hard at work with China's leaders establishing what the role of the military should be, and how and in what ways the PLA should extend its previous missions of deterrence, border defense, and internal security to assert and protect China's emerging interests abroad.

Many of the most sensitive issues that have taken center stage in recent U.S.-China summits, bilateral dialogues, and multilateral meetings have been driven not only by enduring Chinese security interests but also by China's desire to assert and protect these emerging security interests. These include

- reported Chinese cyber espionage cases, most prominently, the reported massive theft of data from the Office of Personnel Management records;

- China's increasing use since 2009 of maritime law enforcement, administrative, military, land reclamation, investment, and other means to assert its still not well-defined sovereignty and resource claims in the disputed areas of the South China Sea;

- the increasingly difficult environment for U.S. businesses in China, especially the legal pressure on foreign high-tech firms to permit government access to proprietary technology and client records; and

- human rights issues, including widespread detentions of human rights attorneys and the arrests of Chinese Uyghurs as part of a crackdown on ethnic separatism, extremism, and social violence.

China's expanding interests also define a large and growing number of arenas in which the United States and China share overlapping but not necessarily identical interests that also make the relationship's challenges increasingly complex. The range of issues on which the two countries actively cooperate continues to widen along with China's global presence. In the past several years, as part of the countries' signature cooperative dialogue—the Strategic and Economic Dialogue—the U.S. State Department has released a list of more than 100 dialogues and other joint projects or endeavors in which China and the United States consult and cooperate. The list truly runs the full range of security, environmental, trade, financial, homeland security, and other areas, and involves engagement across nearly every consequential government agency in both countries. Two noteworthy firsts from 2015 illustrate this trend:

1) The PLA Navy, at the invitation of the U.S. Pacific Command, for the first time took part in the world's largest biennial naval exercise, the Rim of the Pacific exercise (RIMPAC), along with the United States, Japan, India, and many other countries.

2) Homeland Security Secretary Jeh Johnson became the first Department of Homeland Security secretary to visit China, where he met with Chinese representatives and spoke at the Chinese People's Public Security University, China's leading police staff college.

CHINA'S GOVERNANCE PROBLEMS AND THE CHALLENGE TO COOPERATION

Another complex challenge for the U.S.-China relationship is that China's economic and political linkages around the world are so expansive that, for many global issues, it is not sufficient just to have China's public support to address key international problems. Increasingly, China's international partners, including the United States, must also work with Beijing to urge it to develop and strengthen its governance institutions and policy-implementing capacities, and get China to demonstrate sustained resolve in actively supporting and enforcing a wide array of international solutions.

U.S. officials who deal with China find that all too often, even if leading authorities in Beijing nominally support certain international norms, agreements, or arrangements, China's capabilities to enforce, implement, or oversee its commitments may be inadequate. These governance and implementation problems may be sufficient to hold back or undercut international security or enforcement arrangements or other agreements. Notwithstanding the acquiescence of national authorities in Beijing, Chinese local officials, state companies, or Chinese market trends often control more than enough resources or capabilities to undermine some international problem-solving efforts, as long as Beijing does not, or cannot, actively and effectively enforce its international commitments. This is a challenge with respect to a wide range of issues in U.S.-Chinese cooperation and can occur through many channels.

For example, Chinese corporate actors knowingly—or even unconsciously—may sell technology and components to troublesome international actors in disregard of international efforts to cut off these flows. In 2015, the United States and China resumed their dialogue on counterterrorism. One of the central U.S. concerns was urging China to study and pursue international best practices in controlling the precursor chemicals, materials, and technologies for manufacturing improvised explosive devices, in part to prevent the possibility that China's vast computer and chemical industries might become conduits for these items finding their way to extremist groups in countries on or near China's borders. Despite strict on-paper regulations for the handling of dangerous chemicals, Chinese authorities do not believe that these regulations are often enforced adequately—a fact that was horrifically underscored by the tremendous chemical warehouse explosion that took place in the port of Tianjin on August 12, 2015, claiming at least 173 lives. Chinese local officials, moreover, often have far less powerful incentives to enforce regulations on goods that merely exit, or transit through, their areas of jurisdiction.

In another example, Chinese state companies have the financial capacity to undermine international sanctions regimes through their continued purchase of a target country's exports. In 2015, for example, a critical step in enforcing the economic sanctions against Iran and its nuclear program was persuading China and its state petroleum companies to temporarily cut their purchases of petroleum from Tehran. Lurking behind the recent U.S. debate over whether to support the nuclear weapons deal with Iran is the issue of whether China (as well as Russia, India, and other major economic actors) would actively support renewed economic sanctions in the event that U.S. officials called for resuming negotiations with Iran.

The United States and other Chinese partners continue to work with China to "foster the growth of the ineffectual Chinese inspection safety bureaucracies" regarding food, consumer products, pharmaceuticals, and many other products exported from China (Christensen 2015, p. 1). The United States lacks the capacity to inspect all incoming products from China, which raises the importance of building Chinese bureaucracies that can strengthen inspections at the factory.

The United States and China's other economic partners also have a stake in China developing more secure, transparent, and stable financial markets. In this respect, a disturbing aspect of China's summer 2015 stock market collapse was Chinese authorities' reported use of police investigations, threats, harassment of traders, and attacks against journalists for "rumor mongering" to quell the market downturn.

Active Chinese central government support for, and creation of, better intellectual property institutions in China are essential for protecting not only U.S. patent holders but also Chinese inventors and innovators. And while these issues are some of the oldest and most enduring U.S. institutional interests in governance reform, they have been pushed into the background by mounting reports of systematic theft of U.S. foreign corporate intellectual property by state organizations, including Internet theft.

Finally, China's passage in 2016 of a law regarding the management of foreign nongovernmental organizations (NGOs) is also likely to undermine some of the most important private institutional means for actors from the United States and China's other partners to promote improved governance in China on environmental and many other issues. In 2015, U.S. officials on multiple occasions had called for Chinese officials not to adopt tough new regulations that would harm the ability of U.S. and other foreign NGOs to promote better governance and social services in China.

THE CHALLENGES OF BUILDING U.S.-CHINESE "STRATEGIC TRUST"

For many years, Chinese interlocutors—when asked how best to strengthen the U.S.-China relationship—have often told their U.S. partners that the two great powers need to "overcome strategic mistrust" or "build strategic trust." Typically, this call for developing strategic trust has been accompanied by lists of actions that the United States should take that demonstrate respect for China's core national security interests. These proposed actions often relate to rethinking the U.S.-Asian alliance structure, ending U.S. reconnaissance flights near China's territory, decreasing U.S. support to allies and partners locked in tensions with China (recently, in the South China Sea), or lifting restrictions on U.S. technology sales to China.

Notwithstanding these calls for U.S. actions to promote "strategic trust," Chinese officials and analysts, in their writings and interactions with U.S. experts, often mix together at least three schools of thought about the United States' strategic motivations for U.S. actions in the region. These philosophies suggest to this author that many in China's elite will likely struggle to embrace a sense of strategic trust toward the United States, even if it were to make a number of the requested concessions to Chinese interests.

The first school of thought draws on China's sense of historical grievance about its mistreatment by Western powers, including the United States, during its century of semicolonial humiliation.

The second comes from realist or neorealist thinking about international relations theory—a very strong version of "power transition theory," which assumes that established powers such as the United States will be strongly committed to preventing the emergence of rising powers. Some Chinese analysts appear to see this forecast of power transition theory not merely as a theoretical cautionary tale, but as an inevitable historical-empirical fact that has a major impact on U.S. thinking and strategy toward China. Many appear quick to interpret a wide array of U.S. activities—from the U.S. presence in Afghanistan and Pakistan, to the U.S. rebalance to Asia, to the Trans-Pacific Partnership, and human rights advocacy—as being about China, and as tools in a U.S. effort to contain China in a network of adversaries. These assumptions about transitional tensions are certainly a motive for one of Xi Jinping's signature policy initiatives—U.S. approval of what China calls a "new type of great power relationship" between the two countries.

The third school of thought reflects some enduring aspects of Leninist thinking: these include a strong faith that the Chinese Communist Party as an organization is uniquely qualified to strengthen China and its governance and achieve the "China dream." A concern remains that the United States and the world's liberal democratic powers are not merely aspiring to keep China strategically contained as a power—they ultimately aspire to weaken China by bringing down its party-state system, and return China to its self-perceived "sheet of loose sand" weakness of the nineteenth and early twentieth centuries. In particular, this thinking has been discernible in China's reaction to waves of uprisings against authoritarian governments in many other regions of the world—most notably during the 1989–1992 collapse of European Leninism, during the Eurasian "colour revolutions" of 2000–2005, during the Arab Spring uprisings since 2011, and also in U.S. policy toward authoritarianism in countries such as Burma, Thailand, and Sri Lanka. The Arab Spring in particular caused a surprisingly strong "flinch" among Chinese Communist Party leaders, who were concerned that social media could further heighten unrest in China, and who responded with a strong assertion of "social management" systems.

These three schools of thought raise questions about whether the challenges of building strategic trust with China are going to be significantly more different and difficult than might be the case with other emerging powers—powers whose visions of international relations are more narrowly entrenched with traditional realist competitions over greater and lesser international power, and less so with their own individual historical-cultural concerns or global competitions between regime types.

Beyond its potential impact on strategic trust, this third Leninist turn of thought among Chinese leaders and analysts also appears likely to raise challenges to smooth future U.S.-China relations in another area. This concerns the rise over the past 10–15 years of China's efforts to protect the stability of the Chinese Communist system not only on Chinese soil but also increasingly on the sovereign soil of other countries, including the United States. There have been several reported manifestations of this trend: 1) Beijing's insistence that other countries repatriate, extradite, or deport Chinese citizens or noncitizens facing politically tinged charges such as corruption, as well as ethnic and religious minorities fleeing China; 2) China's pressure on other countries not to meet with Uyghur or Tibetan rights activists (including of course the Dalai Lama); and 3) China's apparent increase in the past 15 years of political security investigations abroad by public security and state security officers, such as investigation and research outside the border, or "Operation Foxhunt."

THE TASK OF MOBILIZING U.S. ALLIES AND PARTNERS

A colleague of mine identifies two opposite approaches to U.S. policy toward China and its position in Asia: 1) to get policy toward Asia right, you first need to get policy toward China right, and 2) to get policy toward China right, you first need to get policy toward Asia right.

Mobilizing U.S. relationships with regional allies and strengthening relations with emerging regional partners are the most important challenges facing the United States in its dealings with China—especially allies such as Japan, South Korea, the Philippines, and Australia, non-ally partner Taiwan, and partnerships such as India, Vietnam, Indonesia, Malaysia, and Singapore. Recent Chinese behavior in the South China Sea—notably its land reclamation efforts, oil exploration, and maritime law enforcement operations inside and beyond the Nine-Dash Line—have all created great new opportunities to enhance cooperation with many of these allies and partners in responding to assertive or aggressive Chinese behavior. But managing tensions in the relations between allies or partners remains a challenge—for example, bilateral tensions between Tokyo and Seoul over territorial disagreements and historical issues relating to World War II and Japanese occupation. Being strategic and selective in the management of these partner relations remains a challenge for U.S. policy. U.S relations with Japan, for example, involves continuing to reaffirm U.S. treaty commitments to Tokyo, lauding Japan's positive role as a force for peace, development, and security in the region since WWII, and supporting its potential for expanded security cooperation under the Abe administration policies. But U.S. officials have also judged that effective management of its ties with Japan as part of the United States' East Asia strategy has at times required distancing itself from, for example, some Japanese leaders' views of Japan's WWII conduct, which are still major sources of tension in relations with China, South Korea, and other Asian countries.

The United States will also have to continue to strike a balance between signaling a joint resolve among the United States and its allies and partners to protect common interests in response to Beijing's assertive behavior, attempting to reassure Beijing that the continued alliances and partnerships are not aimed at undermining or encircling China, and continuing to search for new areas where the United States and its allies can enhance nontraditional security cooperation with China in the region on issues such as counterpiracy, antiterrorism, and humanitarian assistance and disaster relief.

THE CHALLENGE AT HOME

Finally, when considering U.S. policies toward China and East Asia, it is necessary not only to "get China right" and "get Asia right" but also to get right several major policy issues here in the United States. A solid long-term policy toward a rising China will also require more focused U.S. attention to China in mass media, classrooms, and elsewhere— discussion that goes beyond an oversimplified debate over "China as partner/China as adversary." U.S. policy has long noted explicitly that the China-U.S. relationship will inevitably combine cooperation and competition. How the United States pursues politics at home has a major impact on its capacity to engage, cooperate with, and compete with China, and to work with its allies and partners to promote and protect regional interests. As one important example, the long-term modernization and development of U.S. Navy capabilities, which are critical to securing U.S. and allied interests in the region, require a stable, long-term approach to budgetary politics. Chinese analysts make note of tensions and obstruction in U.S. governance, and there is evidence to indicate that they interpret it as an important indicator of future U.S. capacity and commitment as a power in the Asia-Pacific.

Note

This chapter is based on remarks made at the 2015–2016 Werner Sichel Lecture Series at Western Michigan University, September 23, 2015. As with the original talk, the views in this chapter are entirely those of the author, and not necessarily those of the CNA Corporation, its corporate officers, or its sponsors. The author is deeply grateful to the WMU Economics Department and the Light Center for Chinese Studies for sponsoring this work.

References

Christensen, Thomas J. 2015. *The China Challenge: Shaping the Choices of a Rising Power*. New York: W.W. Norton.

Tanner, Murray Scot. 2016. "China in 2015: China's Dream, Xi's Party." *Asian Survey* 56(1): 19–33.

Tanner, Murray Scot, and Peter W. Mackenzie. 2015. *China's Emerging National Security Interests and Their Impact on the People's Liberation Army*. Quantico, VA: Marine Corps University Press.

3

Is There a Xi Jinping Model of Economic Reform?

Barry Naughton

University of California, San Diego

Since becoming president of the People's Republic of China in 2012, Xi Jinping has shaken up every aspect of Chinese policy. In the economic realm, Xi laid out an ambitious program of reform in the Third Plenum Resolution of November 2013. However, since that time, progress on economic reform has been slow and uneven. While reform is certainly not dead, there is real reason to question the consistency and effectiveness of Xi's economic policies. This analysis is based on three short steps. First, China is currently undergoing a growth transition. As the period of "miracle growth" ends, nearly every aspect of policy must adapt to a new economic environment. Second, contrary to what we would normally expect under such conditions, Xi Jinping's policy agenda generally relies on a strengthening of government and, especially, party intervention in the society and economy. This orientation is very different from what we would expect for a country moving into middle-income status whose society is far richer and more successful than ever before. Third, the result is a policy regime marked by inconsistent and sometimes contradictory objectives. Xi has attempted to overwhelm these inconsistencies by developing a centralized policy process that gives him very direct control over specific policy outcomes. However, it is unlikely that this approach will succeed in a country as big and complex as China.

THE END OF MIRACLE GROWTH

Between 1978 and 2010, the Chinese economy grew at an average rate of just over 10 percent a year. However, in 2010 the growth rate fell below 8 percent and was 6.7 percent in 2016. This slowdown is not a short-term, cyclical slowdown but, rather, the reflection of a historical turning point. China's miracle growth period was quite similar to that which was experienced earlier by Japan, Korea, and Taiwan. China's growth lasted longer, to be sure, perhaps because some processes of structural change had been delayed during the Cultural Revolution and ended up contributing to the miracle phase of 1978–2010. We learned from the forerunner economies that when the end of the miracle growth era comes, it is often surprisingly abrupt and difficult to manage. This is the case with China as well.

China's economic policy was uniquely well adapted to the high-growth era. Government policy stressed investment, and infrastructure was built out ahead of demand. Since there was a huge reservoir of underutilized labor in the countryside eager to move into the cities, building the roads, factories, airports, and railroads at maximum speed was effective in maintaining high-speed growth. After China entered the World Trade Organization in 2001 with a network of export-oriented factories and regions already in place, there was virtually no limit to the speed with which exports could grow and industrialization could proceed. China could follow the precedents of earlier developing economies, copying and adapting hard and soft technologies, and reproducing systems of infrastructure.

Those days are over. As China moves into middle-income range it is immediately confronted with three fundamental challenges. The first is the end of "Cheap China." As the pool of underutilized labor in the countryside has been drawn down, wages for unskilled workers have risen rapidly. As Figure 3.1 shows, unskilled wages increased particularly rapidly from 2008 to 2013. Since 2014 and 2015, the pace of wage growth has slowed but still remains at 7–8 percent. Despite higher wages, the pace of migration from the countryside has slowed dramatically in recent years. The lower line in Figure 3.1 shows the growth in migrants working outside their home communities. In 2015, the number of cross-country migrants increased only 0.4 percent from the previous year. The increase in wages inevitably means that China's competitiveness in labor-intensive manufactures is eroding. Producers of garments, shoes, and sporting goods are beginning to find that cheaper wages in Vietnam and Bangladesh make it worthwhile moving there, even though overall productivity is still far below that in China. Most importantly,

Figure 3.1 Migrant Worker Earnings and Numbers (real annual growth rates)

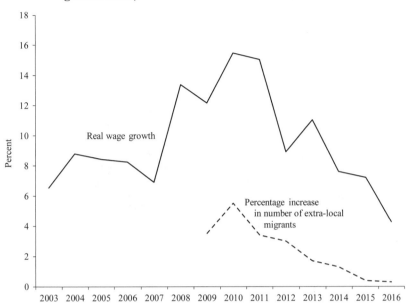

SOURCE: National Bureau of Statistics of China (2016).

these changes in relative costs will likely only strengthen in the future. This fundamental change in labor costs is strongly correlated with the end of the miracle growth era in earlier developing economies such as Japan, Korea, and Taiwan. China, in that sense, is no different.

In one respect, however, China has a distinctive labor force problem. Because of the country's "one-child policy," cohorts of young people entering the labor force today are unusually small. Figure 3.2 is a 2014 population age pyramid. It shows that the age groups graduating from high school and college are already much smaller than the age cohorts just above them, which are the mainstay of the current labor force. Indeed, the cohorts entering the labor force are slightly smaller than the age groups retiring from active labor. The second challenge is thus that since 2010 China's total labor force has plateaued and actually shrunk slightly. The really large decline in China's labor force will not begin until after 2020, but the process has already begun. It is worth

Figure 3.2 2014 Population Age Pyramid: Urban and Rural

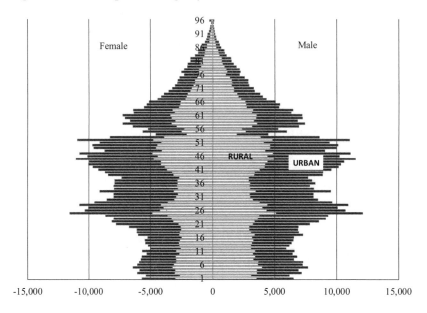

SOURCE: National Census Office (2016).

emphasizing how different this is from the experience of Japan and Korea. In those economies, the end of low-cost labor and the decline in total labor force size were two distinct events separated by decades. For example, Japan's first growth slowdown occurred in 1972, but the Japanese labor force only began to decline in the late 1990s, more than 25 years later. In China, both these changes are occurring at the same time, which means that the two effects reinforce each other, and the adaptation is bound to be especially challenging.

The third challenge is the debt overhang that China has built up over the past 7–8 years. China managed to sustain growth through the global financial crisis. Moreover, since the crisis, policymakers have attempted to keep the growth rate from falling too abruptly. In both cases, one of the primary tools they have used has been to aggressively expand bank lending to keep investment high. For example, one aspect of that debt overhang has been the debt accumulated by local government "funding vehicles." Between 2007 and 2014, that debt jumped from 17 to 35 percent of GDP (Figure 3.3). Debt loads have been increasing in

Figure 3.3 Local Government Funding Platform Debt—Share of GDP

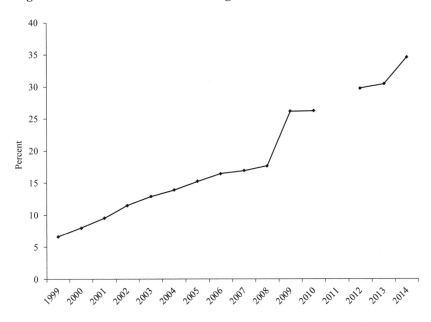

SOURCE: 1990–2010: Gang and Yan (2012). 2012–2014: National Audit Office (2013, 2015).

other areas of the economy as well. While the overall debt level is not yet unsustainable, the trajectory certainly is. China needs to find a way to both slow the increase in debt and restructure the portion of debt that will never be repaid. In a broader sense, sustaining rapid growth by continuously increasing credit simply cannot work indefinitely. Economic policy needs to be adapted to be consistent with an economy growing in the 5–7 percent range.

THE POLICY OBJECTIVES

As described above, the end of China's miracle growth phase echoes and recapitulates what happened earlier in Japan, Korea, and Taiwan. Policymakers in each of those previous miracle growth economies responded in a distinctive fashion, but their responses shared a common feature: they all moved to a lower-investment and a "lighter touch" pattern of government intervention. For Japan and Korea, the heyday of government industrial policy occurred before the slowdown, during the latter half of the miracle growth era. In those countries, industrial policy arguably sustained high growth rates by making sure that the economy could move smoothly into large, capital-intensive heavy-industry sectors. Then, as the miracle growth era ended, both Japan and Korea shifted to a less interventionist industrial policy stance. The logic was that as these countries approached the world technological frontier, it was less likely that government bureaucrats would have an advantage over private actors in foreseeing the next stage of technological or sectoral evolution. Rather than trying to tell businesses how to invest, bureaucrats in Japan and Korea shifted to provide support for private businesses in whatever choices they made. Government investment in research and development, for example, remained high but was increasingly carried out by universities and government research institutes, and it sought to improve society's general knowledge base. Of course, this transition also corresponded with a transition to democracy in both Korea and Taiwan, and in general to more permissive and diverse societies.

Although China has a very different political and economic system from Japan and Korea, the general direction in which China has evolved since 1978 seemed consistent with the earlier evolution of Korea and Japan. Since the 1980s, the Chinese government has stepped back from many aspects of society, and as China became richer, Chinese society became more diverse and tolerant. However, to a remarkable extent, Xi Jinping has sought to reverse this direction. This is most evident in the purely political aspects. Xi Jinping has consolidated his own individual power more rapidly than anyone expected, and he has established his own personal dominance of the political process more thoroughly than most believed possible. The result has been a qualitative change from what had been called the "collegial enlightened dictatorship" of the Deng-Jiang-Hu era toward a more personal rule. Moreover, Xi seeks to infuse the political system with a kind of revivalist spirit and a stronger, top-down discipline. He seeks to project his own charismatic rule to nearly every corner of the system. We can see this objective in Xi's crusade against corruption, in his focus on strong party leadership, and in the ongoing ideological crackdown that is affecting many areas of Chinese society.

In a sense, Xi's policies can be seen as the opposite of those adopted in Japan or Korea, but for structurally similar reasons. As Chinese society has become middle income, the urgency of political goals has faded and materialism and corruption have increased. Rather than acceding to those changes, Xi seeks to reverse them. He has laid out an ambitious agenda that includes Chinese nationalism, assertive and charismatic authoritarian rule, and also economic reform. The question is, do these elements fit together?

Xi Jinping has consistently positioned himself as the architect of a significant economic reform program. The Third Plenum, in November 2013, laid out an economic reform agenda that was bold and broad. Although many parts of the reform resolution were vague—as is normal in top-level China policy documents—a number of concrete commitments were built into the document in order to establish credibility. Moreover, Xi Jinping himself took over a new "leadership small group" (LSG) that had direct authority over the economic reform process. The LSG was an implementation device: the overall reform resolution was broken down into 336 "initiatives" that were farmed out to specialized subgroups under the LSG. The most important of these subgroups from an economic standpoint was the "Economic System and Ecological Civilization Specialized Group." (Paradoxically, it is the only one not headed by a Politburo member.) This specialized group was given the responsibility for 118 out of the 336 total initiatives. Headed by Xi Jinping's close economic counselor, Liu He, this specialized group serves as a kind of economic secretariat, charged with implementing Xi's policy preferences.

This implementation process is a significant departure from past Chinese practice. Since the early 1980s it has been standard practice for economic policy to be run directly out of the governmental State Council by the premier. Successive premiers Zhao Ziyang, Zhu Rongji, and Wen Jiabao all controlled day-to-day economic decision making and placed their own personal stamp on economic policy. Under Xi Jinping, however, most of the crucial economic decisions relating to economic reform have been pulled back into the specialized group.

These changes mean that Xi Jinping's personal stamp is inevitably on the economic reform process. Xi has laid out a set of goals that shape and constrain the economic reform process. He has identified his own personal leadership with economic reform. The policy process has been changed in important respects that reflect Xi's wishes. The success or failure of economic reforms in China today, therefore, depend directly on whether the "Xi Jinping model" of economic reform is a reality or an illusion.

2015: THE ANNUS HORRIBILIS OF ECONOMIC REFORM

Reforms came out of the gate quickly after the Third Plenum in November 2013. There was a great deal of activity during 2014 that seemed to be focused on moving the reform process ahead in productive ways. However, during 2015, these initiatives met with unexpected problems. Indeed, it is reasonable to say that in 2015 economic reforms failed. We can see this in three major reform initiatives:

1) restructuring local government debt,

2) opening the stock market, and

3) state enterprise reform.

Each of these initiatives went off track in 2015. Whether they can be revived is an open question.

Restructuring Local Government Debt

Beginning in 2014, the Minister of Finance, Lou Jiwei, laid out an ambitious program of local debt restructuring. Even more impressive, in Lou's vision, debt restructuring was merely the first phase of a broader fiscal system reorganization. After weaning local governments off their dependence on debt, Lou believed he would be able to create appropriate conditions for an across-the-board overhaul of the fiscal system. In his original vision, this overhaul would be carried out in three years, from 2014 to 2016.

Following Lou's program, overall government debt was audited and officially registered as of December 2014. The intention was to cap debt at this year-end level and then begin to transform debt into new, local government "municipal bonds," which would be sold into the marketplace at an interest rate that reflected the relative creditworthiness of different local governments. This bold vision not only comprised restructuring fiscal relations but also the creation of a new fixed-income market that would contribute to China's financial reforms as well. However, this initial program of debt restructuring failed. When the first batch of bonds created by Jiangsu Province was offered to the market in April 2015, buyers and sellers were unable to agree on an interest rate. If this were to be a truly market-based sale of debt, buyers wanted substantially higher rates as compensation for their risk than the Jiangsu government was willing to pay. The government was forced to withdraw the offer.

The program was reformulated and converted essentially into a bailout. The mechanism was that the banks, which held the existing debt, were now pressured to buy the new municipal bonds. While a fiction was maintained that the interest rate was to be "mutually agreed," banks were led to understand that the appropriate interest rate should be similar to that of central government bonds—that is, extremely low. The banks were given some sweeteners to induce their compliance, but of course these predominantly state-owned banks could not refuse a central government policy initiative in any case. Under these new circumstances, local debt restructuring proceeded quickly. An initial quota of 1 trillion RMB was rapidly converted and, over the course of 2015, slightly more than 3 trillion were sold. Further debt restructuring continued, and even accelerated, and in 2016, an additional 5 trillion RMB in debt was converted.

Debt restructuring achieved some partial objectives, since it lowered interest rates and reduced the debt servicing burden on local governments. In that sense, it was not a complete failure. However, the objective of debt restructuring is not simply to reduce financial burdens but also to place the system on a new, more sustainable basis. A restructuring that is little more than a bailout sends a message to local governments that fiscally reckless behavior will be accepted and, indeed, may be costless. Of course, the Ministry of Finance has argued that local governments are no longer allowed to take on any new debt, but it remains to be seen whether this prohibition is credible. Moreover, the broader Ministry of Finance program of fiscal restructuring is in shambles. Major new taxes have not been introduced, and the restructuring of central-local relations is still far over the horizon.

Stock Market Reform

Beginning in 2014, Chinese policymakers laid out an ambitious reform of equity markets. Two measures exemplified this reform. First, all qualified firms were allowed to be listed on the market. This was a dramatic departure from past procedure in which only a select few firms, individually approved by the securities regulator, could list on the Shanghai Stock Exchange. The old system had unduly favored state-owned enterprises and led to delays, inefficiency, and corruption. Moreover, the old system had repeatedly tempted the government to use the pace of new listings as a tool to manipulate the stock markets' overall level. When the market was sluggish, policymakers would suspend new listings, so market participants could be confident that there would be no liquidity shocks. Indeed, new listings had been suspended for years before 2014. By taking steps to open up the listing process, the government was committing to a much more market-driven stock market, even at the risk of allowing short-term downward pressure on the market. Second, the Chinese stock market was de facto opened up to international investors for the first time. The creation of the Hong Kong–Shanghai Capital Connect allowed Hong Kong brokers to buy and sell shares on the Shanghai market up to a certain relatively generous quota. Since any international financial institution can maintain a Hong Kong subsidiary, this was a tentative and gradualist, but still unmistakeable, opening of the Shanghai market to foreign investment.

The impact of these initial reform measures was swept away by a huge boom and bust in the Chinese stock market. The Chinese market soared to a peak of 5,166 on June 12, 2015. From there, it wobbled and then crashed, amid something close to panic, to a low point of 3,507 on July 8. When the market plummeted, China's leaders lost their nerve. Beginning on July 5, Premier Li Keqiang presided over a series of meetings designed to bail out the stock market. An existing organization, the China Securities Finance Corporation, was provided with unlimited liquidity to buy up blue-chip (or, rather, red-chip) stocks. Remarkably, despite this massive intervention, the market continued to drop for another three days before finally stabilizing. With substantial direct government ownership now complementing already large state enterprise holdings, the stock market ended up further away than ever from genuine marketization. Moreover, public funds had once again been used to bail out politically influential groups.

From this account, it might seem that Premier Li Keqiang was the crucial actor in the stock market fiasco, but that is not the case. The entire political leadership, including Xi Jinping, had been complicit in statements that directly or indirectly encouraged the stock market bubble. Xi Jinping was widely quoted in Weibo (Chinese Twitter) as having advocated much higher market valuations. While there is no official source for these comments, the Chinese government could easily have denied or deleted them, had it chosen to do so. It is inconceivable that Xi Jinping did not either instruct Li Keqiang to intervene or at least signal his support for such intervention. After the bailout, new listings were once again suspended. The Hong Kong–Shanghai stock connect was still intact, but interest from overseas investors quickly evaporated. Not only did the market still seem to be in a bear mode, but the added risk of unpredictable government policy was too great for most foreign investors to take. A later episode in January 2016 merely accentuated these fears. As of mid-2016, government holdings in the stock market were still large, and the overall Shanghai index was languishing at around 3,000 points, which is to say below what it was after the summer of 2015 crash. The overhang of government holdings deters new investors from entering the market.

State Enterprise Reform

State-owned enterprise (SOE) reform started strong after the Third Plenum (November 2013) resolution. It was given high priority in the resolution, which also generated excitement because it introduced a number of potential innovative approaches. These included an expanded role for "mixed ownership," new investment funds that would manage government wealth, and a role for employee share owning. However, the attempt to translate these innovative ideas into reality was quickly stifled. Disagreements about basic definitions and philosophy prevented progress. Then, in the summer of 2014, the reform LSG made several decisions that thoroughly upended the stalled (but gradual) SOE reform process. Most strikingly, the LSG approved a limitation on the salaries of SOE managers. This policy, designed to bring SOE managers' salaries in line with those of bureaucrats at a similar level, reduced salaries in listed state-owned enterprises and dramatically lowered the salaries of managers at Chinese state-owned banks. The abrupt adoption of these salary caps underlined the extent to which Xi Jinping was seeking to achieve mixed objectives in his approach to SOEs.

Perhaps as a result of this confusion, at the same meeting a new specialized "SOE Reform LSG" was created to hammer out a compromise. However, this group—whose composition must have been endorsed by Xi Jinping—was headed by a long-time veteran of the economic bureaucracy, Vice-Premier Ma Kai. Moreover, it was staffed by the head of the existing agency that controlled SOEs, namely, the State Asset Supervision and Administration Commission (SASAC). This choice was unfortunate, to say the least. The whole purpose of SOE reform was to replace SASAC, which had evolved out of earlier government agencies, with a mixed mandate of incremental improvements to state firm management. However, if there were to be a substantial improvement in the way state ownership was exercised, it would almost certainly have to involve the creation of new kinds of investment funds. By handing the design of SOE reform over to SASAC leaders, Xi Jinping effectively ensured that the creation of new investment funds would be controlled by the insiders in charge of existing institutions. SASAC leaders would understandably seek to limit change, or at least make sure that any reorganization occurred under their own direct control.

It took one year for the SOE Reform LSG to draft its program. When that program finally emerged in September 2015, it was marked by contradictions and compromises and was met with a general sense of disappointment. Underlying this disappointment was the realization that SASAC had opted for an extremely gradual process of insider-controlled change. The 2013 reform resolution had called for the creation of new "State Capital Investment and Operation Companies." Much of the previous deadlock had been due to competing conceptions of what those companies should do. One version of the investment companies, proposed by the Ministry of Finance, held that those companies should manage state firms as purely financial assets. The investment funds would seek to maximize the financial returns of their holdings, potentially by having competing managers evaluated by the return they generate. This conception evoked comparisons with successful sovereign wealth funds, such as Singapore's Temasek. The alternative version of the investment companies, proposed by SASAC, stressed their utility as development agencies. After the SOE reform document was published, SASAC announced that it would convert two of its existing companies into "State Capital Investment and Operation Companies." These companies were designed to have specific developmental objectives and engage in hands-on restructuring. Thus, from the standpoint of the firms, the new ownership agencies that emerged from the SOE reform process were really not much better than the old SASAC control.

It was clear that Xi Jinping's vision of SOE reform included many competing objectives. Related to his anticorruption drive, Xi clearly wanted to improve oversight of SOE management. Paralleling his overall stress on Communist Party leadership, Xi insisted that Communist Party committees in the enterprise should have first right to discuss important strategic decisions on the enterprise. Overall, this meant that Xi Jinping was asking for SOEs to be given new tasks and to be subject to new oversight, even while telling them they should be given more autonomy to work as market-oriented entities.

The above account oversimplifies the complex process of SOE reform. On the positive side, the long, stalled agenda of converting all SOEs into corporations, with an established board of directors, has been given new momentum. In addition, firms are to be categorized according to whether they are in a competitive market environment or primarily a public service operation. In addition, many different provinces are experimenting with accelerating SOE reform. These positive elements may well improve the conduct and performance of China's SOEs in the medium term. But in 2015 it was clear that dramatic progress in SOE reform had not been achieved, and this was because of the conflicting goals and obligations placed on SOEs by top political leadership without a dramatic push toward a stronger market orientation. The SOE reform that emerged from this jumble of objectives is unlikely to be a real reform at all.

CONCLUSION AND EVALUATION

By the end of 2015, all three of the reform initiatives described in the previous section had failed. While the government continues to give verbal support to the goals of the Third Plenum, it has tacitly acknowledged the failure of the program by shifting emphasis to a new reform initiative called "Supply-Side Structural Reform." First floated at the end of 2015, this complex new initiative clearly represents a new approach. Policymakers have shown some inclination to resume progress in equity and fiscal system reform, and 2016 was designated as the first year of implementation of SOE reform (taking the September 2015 document as the definitive elaboration of the program). However, as of 2016, progress in these areas has been extremely modest.

What can we conclude from this situation? First, there is a Xi Jinping model—a model of economic reform that follows from his commitment to top-down, personalized rule. Xi declares a bold set of objectives, but they are not in the form of a broad, philosophical commitment to a new type of system; rather, they represent a wish list of objectives Xi would like to achieve from the existing system. In order to achieve those objectives, Xi sets up a new top-down implementation process.

At the beginning of the Xi administration, a number of analysts suggested that Xi Jinping's efforts to concentrate political power on its own hands were a necessary prelude to dramatic economic reforms. According to this view, entrenched interest groups had made incremental reform increasingly difficult in China. Therefore, an authoritative policymaker would need to concentrate power first and then push through with reforms. The experience of 2015 indicates that this view has very little explanatory power. On the contrary, concentration of power in the hands of just a few may even retard the reform process. Xi's personalized style leads him to impose contradictory demands on the reform process. This in turn leads to sometimes abrupt about-faces in the tasks set for other policymakers, which is exemplified in each of the reform areas discussed in this chapter. Xi's sudden moves to cap SOE salaries, abandon high-quality municipal bond markets, and intervene to save the stock market all had dire implications for the overall reform process.

The new organs Xi set up to implement these policies have also not worked well. These new agencies do not themselves have direct implementation capabilities—they can talk about bold reforms, but when it comes to actually designing a reform process, they end up falling back on the same government agencies that cater to interest groups. This is shown by the fate of SOE reform in 2015–2016. There really is no benefit to concentrating power if that newly concentrated power needs to compromise with existing interest groups to achieve institutional change.

Finally, there may be a deeper contradiction between the requirements of this stage of economic reform and the exercise of authority by a single individual. To be sure, an authoritative leader may be helpful in the first stage of reform, adapting to crises and throwing off old constraints. However, at a certain point, market-oriented reforms require the authoritative leader to step back and allow market forces to work without constraint. China today has developed a vigorous market economy—the greatest need at this stage is for independent regulatory and financial institutions, which have not been a prominent part of the Xi Jinping reform package. Therefore, the year 2015 provided little support for the idea that an authoritative Xi Jinping leadership can contribute effectively to the economic reform process.

With the failure of reform initiatives in 2015, China has been left without a good strategy to cope with the end of the miracle growth period. In a general sense, everyone understands that the "new normal" requires greater innovation, stronger orientation to domestic consumers, and the shift to a service economy. Economic reform is ideally suited to facilitate those structural shifts. Without a successful program of economic reform, Xi's China will be forced to rely on endless programs of government investment supported by an ultimately unsustainable increase in credit and debt.

References

Gang, Fan, and Yan Lv. 2012. "Fiscal Prudence and Growth Sustainability: An Analysis of China's Public Debts." *Asian Economic Policy Review* 7(2): 202–220.

National Audit Office. 2013. "Report on Audit of Local Government Debt." Beijing: National Audit Office. http://www.audit.gov.cn/n4/n19/c45343/content.html (accessed April 28, 2016).

———. 2015. "Report on Audit of Local Government Debt." Beijing: National Audit Office. http://www.audit.gov.cn/n4/n19/c45343/content.html (accessed April 28, 2016).

4

Understanding the Major Threats to China's Economic Growth

Wing Thye Woo
University of California, Davis
and Sunway University

Predictions of gloom and doom for China have a long tradition among economists. In the mid-1990s, Nicholas Lardy of the Peterson Institute for International Economics started highlighting the de facto insolvency of the Chinese banking system with the implication that a bank run leading to financial sector collapse (which would then be likely to send the economy into a tailspin) was a strong possibility in the medium term.[1] The twenty-first century began with the claim by Gordon Chang (2001) that China's imminent accession to the World Trade Organization (WTO) would cause such widespread unemployment within China's already alienated population that China's economic and political systems would collapse.

These two dire predictions have turned out to be wrong. China, in fact, accelerated its annual GDP growth to double-digit rates after 2001. Nicholas Lardy was wrong because while the banks were indeed bankrupt, the Chinese government, which owned them, was not and could hence afford to bail out the banks when necessary. The fiscal strength of the government made it irrational for depositors to contemplate a bank run. Gordon Chang was wrong because the WTO membership quickened the pace of job creation in China by greatly increasing the volume of foreign direct investment inflow. The WTO membership made China more attractive to foreign direct investment because it guaranteed the access of Chinese goods to the U.S. market by eliminating the need for China to get the most-favored-nation (MFN) status annually from the U.S. Congress (McKibbin and Woo 2003).

The literature on China's future growth became pessimistic again in the mid-2000s. One of the most astute analysts in China, Minxin Pei

(2006), argues that China is now in a *trapped transition* that is described as "a transformative phase in which half-finished reforms have transferred power to new, affluent elites" who are using crony capitalism to generate high economic growth that is not sustainable. He believes that meaningful reform to ensure continued high growth is improbable.[2]

Pei's pessimism about the inevitable exhaustion of China's growth momentum has been shared by another leading China scholar, Yasheng Huang (2008). In Huang's contrarian assessment, China in 1999 was actually less capitalistic than China in 1989. He asserted that the administration of Jiang Zemin and Zhu Rongji, which ended in March 2003, had reversed the march toward capitalism by systematically promoting the growth of large state-owned firms in the urban areas and suppressing the activities of the privately owned small and medium firms in the countryside. Huang has attributed the deterioration in income distribution across classes and across regions to this reoccupation of the commanding heights of the economy by state-controlled companies (often in cahoots with foreign private companies), and the intensification of discrimination against the domestic private firms. Because Huang believes (very reasonably, based on international experience) that the state-controlled firms are intrinsically less innovative than the domestic private firms, he concludes that China will be unable to move on to the next stage of economic development in the near future (at least not before India does so).[3]

THE ROUGH ROAD TO PROSPERITY

China's economy has been like a speeding car—in just 30 years, China has gone from one of the world's poorest countries to the second-largest economy. It is not surprising, then, to hear more glowingly optimistic assessments of China's future than dismissively pessimistic ones. For example, O'Neill et al. (2005) of Goldman Sachs predict that China's GDP will surpass that of the United States in 2040 even after assuming that China's GDP growth rate will slow down steadily from its annual average of 10 percent in the 1979–2005 period to 3.8 percent in the 2030–2040 period.[4]

A good guide on how one should regard the competing optimistic and pessimistic literature is found in the discussions of the Sixth Plenum of the Sixteenth Central Committee of the Communist Party of China (CPC) that concluded on October 11, 2006. The Sixth Plenum passed a resolution to commit the CPC to establish a harmonious society by 2020. The obvious implication from this commitment is that the major social, economic, and political trends within China might not lead to a harmonious society or, at least not fast enough.

Among the disharmonious features mentioned in the fifth paragraph of the "resolutions of the CPC Central Committee on major issues regarding the building of a harmonious socialist society" were the serious imbalance in the social and economic development across (and within each of) China's 31 provinces, worsening population and environmental problems, grossly inadequate social safety nets and medical care system, and serious corruption. The harmonious socialist society proposed by the Sixth Plenum would encompass a democratic society under the rule of law; a society based on equality and justice; an honest and caring society; a stable, vigorous, and orderly society; and a society in which humans live in harmony with nature.

What is the origin of the CPC's decision to change its primary focus from "economic construction" to "social harmony"? And why include a target date of 2020? I believe that this switch in emphasis from "economic construction" to "social harmony" occurs because the Hu-Wen leadership understands that the political legitimacy of CPC rule rests largely on maintaining an economic growth rate that is high enough to keep unemployment low, and also a growth pattern that diffuses the additional income widely enough. Specifically, the Hu-Wen leadership recognizes that without accelerated institutional reforms and new major policy initiatives on a broad front, the 1978–2005 policy framework, which had produced an average annual GDP growth rate of almost 10 percent, is at odds with environmental sustainability and with international concerns about China's persistent trade imbalances. More importantly, unless their new policies could produce significant improvements in social harmony by 2020, social instability would reduce China's economic growth and thus make the leadership of CPC in Chinese politics unsustainable.

Returning to the analogy of China's economy being like a speeding car, the Hu-Wen leadership saw that the car could crash because there were three high-probability failures that might occur and cause an economic collapse: 1) hardware failure, 2) software failure, and 3) power supply failure.

A hardware failure refers to the breakdown of an economic mechanism, a development that is analogous to the collapse of the chassis of the car. Probable hardware failures include a banking crisis that causes a credit crunch that, in turn, dislocates production economy-wide, and a budget crisis that necessitates reductions in important infrastructure and social expenditure (and possibly generates high inflation and balance of payments difficulties as well).

A software failure refers to a flaw in governance that creates frequent widespread social disorders that disrupt production economy-wide and discourage private investment. This situation is like a car crash that resulted from a fight among the people inside the speeding car. Software failures could come from the present high-growth strategy creating so much inequality and corruption that it generates severe social unrest, which dislocates economic activities, and from the state not being responsive enough to rising social expectations, hence causing social disorder.

A power supply failure refers to the economy being unable to move forward because it hits either a natural limit or an externally imposed limit—a situation that is akin, respectively, to the car running out of gas or to the car smashing into a barrier erected by an outsider. Examples of power supply failures are an environmental collapse, such as climate change or a collapse in China's exports because of a trade war. In a sense, the repair of a power supply failure is more difficult than either the repair of a hardware failure or the repair of a software failure because a large part of the repair has to be undertaken in collaboration with other countries. For example, the lowering of trade barriers requires China to negotiate with other countries, and the reversal of environmental damage could require an advance in scientific understanding—an outcome that is more likely to occur when the entire scientific talent in China and the rest of the world is focused on the task.

A discussion of the many events that could make China's high growth unsustainable is beyond the scope of this chapter. This analysis will focus on one or two of the most likely precipitating events in each class of failures. The following section identifies the weakening of China's fiscal position by nonperforming loans (NPLs) in the state banks as the likely type of hardware failure that would occur. The next section discusses the outbreak of social disorder as the likely type of software failure. For power supply failures, the two most likely ones are the erection of trade barriers against China's exports (discussed in the next three sections), and an environmental collapse, especially a shortage of water (discussed in the final section).

Hardware Failure

Among doomsayers, one favorite mechanism for the forthcoming collapse of an economy is the inevitable fiscal crisis of the state. It is noteworthy that this fiscal mechanism is used by doomsayers of all stripes. The Marxist economist James O'Connor (1973) predicted that the dynamics of capitalist America would precipitate a fiscal crisis that would destabilize the economy completely. In turn, the capitalist lawyer Gordon Chang (2001) predicted that a fiscal crisis could trigger the event in the unavoidable disintegration of socialist China.

This fixation on a large negative fiscal shock as a totally destructive systemic shock is understandable because fiscal imbalance is the proximate cause in most crises. The reason is that the state budget is often faced with the task of defusing the cumulative tensions unleashed by deeper, more fundamental social processes. To a first approximation, fiscal capacity is a fundamental determinant of system stability because economic sustainability depends on the ability to cover production costs, and political viability depends on the ability to reward one's supporters and to pay off one's enemies.

The reality in many cases is that fiscal sustainability is the prerequisite for both economic sustainability and political viability, and that economic sustainability and political viability are intricately linked and mutually reinforcing. To see the mutual interdependence of the two, one only has to recall the many times that near-bankrupt governments have been driven out of power after raising the prices of a subsidized item like food, petrol, or foreign exchange.[5] One could indeed go so far as to say that the degree of economic and political resilience of a state can be measured by the state's ability to cover an unexpected, prolonged increase in expenditure or an unanticipated, protracted shortfall in revenue.

An OECD (2006) report has raised grave concerns about China's fiscal management.

> China's officially reported spending figures reflect only about three-quarters of total government spending. Extra-budgetary spending, social security outlays and central government bond financing of local projects are not part of the official budget. Notwithstanding recent reforms, the government remains overly exposed to extra-budget and off-budget activities, which make public expenditures difficult to plan and control and which impair their accountability and transparency. Contingent liabilities have been a major source of unplanned spending and pose perhaps the greatest risk to the controllability of future expenditure. (p. 10)

Fiscal sustainability is central to economic management. This can be seen in the two fiscal targets that the original Growth and Stability Pact of the countries in the eurozone specified for its members to meet: 1) the consolidated government budget deficit should not exceed 3 percent of GDP except in case of unusually severe downturn, and 2) the debt-GDP ratio should be brought down to 60 percent or lower.

The very aggressive fiscal-monetary policy mix undertaken by the government to combat the global financial crisis that hit China at the end of the third quarter of 2008 has now created an NPL ratio that the investment house CLSA has put in the range of 15–19 percent, compared to the official estimate of 1.6 percent. A recapitalization of the banking system is inevitable.

The important question is, how many more rounds of bank recapitalization can China afford without generating a fiscal crisis? The simple fact is that fiscal sustainability lies at the heart of whether a banking crisis would actually occur. As long as the state is perceived to be able and willing to bail out the state-owned banks (SOBs), depositors would retain their confidence in the SOBs regardless of the actual state of their balance sheets. The current value of the debt-to-GDP ratio is not a good indicator of the sustainability of the existing fiscal policy regime; a better indicator would involve working out the evolution of the debt-to-GDP ratio over time.

To put the issue formally, the evolution of the debt-to-GDP ratio as given by

$$d\,(\ln[\text{Debt/GDP}])\,/\,d\,t = r + [\text{GDP/Debt}] \times [f + b] - y$$

where

r = real interest rate on government debt

f = primary fiscal deficit rate [(state expenditure excluding debt service – state revenue) / GDP]

b = NPL creation rate [(change in NPL in SOBs) / GDP]

y = trend growth rate of real GDP

As long as $y > r$, then the debt-to-GDP ratio will have a steady-state value that is nonzero when sum of $(f + b) > 0$. Specifically,

$$(\text{Debt/GDP})_{\text{steady-state}} = (f + b) / (y - r) \text{ when } y > r$$

China appears to belong to this case because its post-1978 annual growth rate has averaged 9.4 percent, its growth rate in the next 10 years is likely to be above 8 percent; and the real interest rate has been about 4 percent. For the generation of likely future scenarios, I will make the conservative assumptions that y is 8 percent, f is 1 percent, and r is 6 percent.[6] It is difficult to predict b, the rate that banks would generate NPLs, because it depends on the type of banking reform undertaken. If no meaningful reforms are undertaken, then b is likely to remain at the historic value of 6 percent.

So, conditional on the effectiveness of reforming the SOBs, the steady-state ratio is

$$(\text{Debt/GDP})_{\text{steady-state}} = 350 \text{ percent when } b = 6 \text{ percent}$$

$$(\text{Debt/GDP})_{\text{steady-state}} = 200 \text{ percent when } b = 3 \text{ percent}$$

$$(\text{Debt/GDP})_{\text{steady-state}} = 100 \text{ percent when } b = 1 \text{ percent}$$

The noteworthy finding from the above scenarios is that China will produce a level of $(\text{Debt/GDP})_{\text{steady-state}}$ that is high by international experience despite the optimistic assumptions that long-run growth rate is 8 percent, that b will be lowered from 6 percent of GDP to 1 percent. The most optimistic outcome is still two-thirds larger than what the European Union has set to be the "safe" debt-GDP target (60 percent) for its members. The banking system has made China vulnerable to a fiscal crisis, even though there is a theoretical steady-state level for the debt-to-GDP ratio. Of course, the creation of NPLs cannot be attributed entirely to the SOBs; their chief customers, the embezzlement-ridden and inefficiency-ridden state-owned enterprises (SOEs), deserve an equal share of the blame (see Woo [2001]; Woo et al. [1994]).

The important point from this second fiscal feature is that the present ongoing recapitalization of the SOBs is the last time that the government can afford to recapitalize the SOBs, and possibly the last time that the government can do so without upsetting confidence in the financial markets about the soundness of China's fiscal regime.

How difficult is it to stop losses in the SOBs in order to ensure fiscal sustainability? The solution lies in imposing a hard budget constraint on the SOBs. SOB managers must be convinced that the present recapitalization is indeed the last free supper (which the 1998 recapitalization was announced to be), and that their compensation and promotion will depend only on the profitability of the SOBs relative to the profitability of private banks.

At the same time, the prudential supervision and monitoring of bank operations will have to be strengthened to prevent asset stripping and discourage reckless investments fostered by the asymmetrical reward system under the soft budget constraint.[7] The operations of SOBs could be further improved by bringing in foreign strategic investors who would be part of the management team, and by removing the influence of the local governments on bank operations.

Another way to harden the budget constraint faced by the SOBs is to privatize some of their branches and use the performance of the new private banks to gauge the performance of the remaining SOBs. The privatization of some branches will also help convince the SOB managers that the government is indeed serious about the present SOB recapitalization.

Software Failure

A successful market economy requires its regulatory institutions to have the prerequisite scientific understanding to determine whether a patent case involves real technological innovation. China's strategy of incremental reform, combined with the fact that institution building is a time-consuming process, means that many of its regulatory institutions are either absent or ineffective. The results have been governance failures on many fronts, of which the most well-known recent governance failures are the violations against the welfare of consumers and workers.

There have been significant regulatory failures in keeping China's food supply and pharmaceutical products safe. The misuse of chemicals to lower production costs has resulted in the addition of poisonous substitutes into toothpaste (Barboza and Bogdanich 2007; Bogdanich 2007), cough medicine (Bogdanich and Hooker 2007), and animal feed (Barboza 2007a; Barboza and Barrionuevo 2007); the application of lead paint to children's toys (Barboza and Story 2007; *Financial Times* 2007; Lipton and Barboza 2007);[8] and the overemployment of antifungals and antibacterials in fish farming (Barboza 2007b; Martin 2007a). Most of these abuses received enormous attention because these items were exported to other countries, and their harmful effects were reported widely in the international press.[9] Clearly, Chinese consumers have been suffering much more from such types of malfeasance, the scope of which has not been realized because of the considerable press censorship in China (Barboza 2007c).

Dereliction in duty by government officials is the fundamental reason for such governance failures. The most well-known recent case was the conviction of Zheng Xiaoyu, the former director of China's food and drug safety agency, for accepting bribes to approve production licenses for pharmaceutical companies and food companies. Such dereliction in official oversight has resulted in

> tens of thousands of people [being] sickened or killed every year as a result of rampant counterfeiting of drugs, and tainted and substandard food and drugs. For instance, last year 11 people died in China with an injection tainted by a poisonous chemical. Six people died and 80 others fell ill after taking an antibiotic that had been produced . . . with a substandard disinfectant. Small drug makers in China have long been accused of manufacturing phony or substandard drugs and marketing them to the nation's hospitals and pharmaceutical companies. And mass poisonings involving tainted food products are common. (Barboza 2007d)

There have also been significant regulatory failures in the treatment of labor, especially in the areas of occupational safety and wage payments. One of the most recent horrifying accounts involved forced labor of kidnapped children in the brick kilns of Shanxi and Henan provinces (Buckley 2007; *China Daily* 2007). Reuters (2007) reports that "as many as 1,000 children may have been sold into slave labor in central China." This deplorable affair was exposed partly "because of an open letter posted online by a group of 400 fathers appealing for help in tracking missing sons they believed were sold to kiln boss" (*New York Times* 2007). A parent visiting the brick kilns in her quest to find her son found that the local police were not only unwilling to help but also demanded bribes instead (French 2007). In one case, the brick kiln was owned by the son of the village Party secretary (*New York Times* 2007).

Perhaps, the two most dismaying revelations from the news reports on the brick kiln slavery are that this sad state of affairs had been going on for a decade;[10] and the "forced labor and sexual exploitation have increased as the trend in human trafficking in China has taken a turn for the worst" (Zhouqiong 2007). Yin Jianzhong, the senior official at the Ministry of Public Security who identified the worsening trend in human trafficking in China, recognized a reason for the negative development to be "the loopholes in the legal and labor systems. . . . [Specifically,] the Criminal Law on human trafficking protects women and children only and leaves out grown-up and teen males. It doesn't have provisions for punishing those trafficking people for forced labor or prostitution" (Zhouqiong 2007). The fact that such legal loopholes exist supports our contention that the main cause behind the administrative failures in China is the "dereliction of duty by government officials."[11]

Inadequate institutions of governance are not the only cause of social tensions in China, however. The present economic development strategy, despite its ability to generate high growth, also generates high social tensions because, in the last 10 years, it has had great difficulty further reducing extreme poverty and significantly improving the rural-urban income distribution and the regional income distribution (see Démurger et al. [2002] and Woo et al. [2004]). In the first half of the 1990s, the $1.00 poverty rate (i.e., the proportion of rural population receiving a daily income of $1.00 or less) dropped rapidly from 31.3 percent in 1990 to 15.0 percent in 1996. But as Figure 4.1 shows, in the following six years the decline was only 5 percentage points. The $1.00 poverty rate stayed in the 10–12 percent rate in the 1998–2003 period, even though the GDP growth rate averaged 8.5 percent annually. It was only after the sustained large-scale effort to develop western

Figure 4.1 Proportion of Rural Population under Different Specifications of the Poverty Line

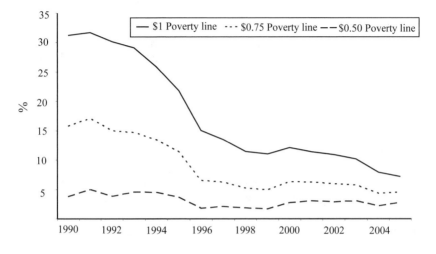

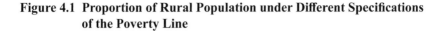

NOTE: The 1990–1997 data are from World Bank (2001, Annex 1 Table 3), and the post-1997 numbers are computed by Ximing Yue (private communication).

China began in 2001 and the post-2002 rise in the GDP growth rate to 10 percent or higher that the $1.00 poverty rate dropped to 7.9 percent in 2004 and then to 7.2 percent in 2005.

However, the progress in poverty alleviation in the last decade is considerably much less impressive when the poverty line is lowered. The $0.75 poverty rate stayed unchanged from 1998 (4.6 percent) to 2005 (4.2 percent); and the $0.50 poverty rate actually increased from 1.9 percent in 1998 to 2.8 percent in 2005. In short, the higher growth rate in the 2003–2005 period did not cause income to trickle down to the poorest 5 percent of the rural population, and hence caused income inequality to worsen.

In the 1985–1987 period, China's Gini coefficient was below 0.3.[12] According to a report in the official *China Daily* in 2005:

> China's income gap widened in the first quarter of the year [2005], with 10 percent of the nation's richest people enjoying 45 percent of the country's wealth. . . . China's poorest 10 percent had only 1.4 percent of the nation's wealth. . . . No precise Gini coefficient was provided [by the state statistical agency], but state press reports in

recent weeks said the value was more than 0.48 and approaching
0.5. . . . Most developed European nations tend to have coefficients
of between 0.24 and 0.36, while the United States has been above
0.4 for several decades. (*China Daily* 2005)

The Asian Development Bank (2007) recently conducted a study
of income inequality in 22 Asian countries over the 1992–2004 period.
For 2004, only Nepal had a Gini coefficient (47.30 percent) that was
higher than China's (47.25). However, in 2004, China's income ratio
of the richest 20 percent to the poorest 20 percent (11.37) was highest
in Asia—significantly higher than the next highest income ratio (9.47
for Nepal). China is probably the most unequal country in Asia today.

Table 4.1 presents the income inequality in China within the international context. China's income inequality today is generally lower
than in Latin America but generally higher than in Africa. The steady
increase in China's income inequality since 1985 raises the possibility that China is heading toward the Latin American degree of income
inequality.

The reason that doing more of the same economic policies in today's
China will not produce the same salubrious results of quick reduction
in poverty and slow increase in inequality as in the early phases of economic reform is because the development problems have changed. In
the first phase of economic development, the provision of more jobs
(through economic deregulation) was enough to lower poverty significantly. Many of the people who are still poor require more than just job
opportunities; they first need an infusion of assistance (e.g., empower-
ing them with human capital through education and health interventions) in order to seize these job opportunities. Effective governance for
equitable growth has now become even more challenging, and so the
probability of improving social harmony has been diminished.

Furthermore, the present mode of economic development generates immense opportunities for embezzlement of state assets, seizure
of farmlands for industrial development, and corruption because of the
absence of effective mechanisms to supervise government employees
(see Woo [2001]). These features certainly make social harmony hard
to sustain.

The data on social unrest are consistent with the hypothesis of rising social disharmony. First, the incidences of public disorder, or *social
incidents*, have risen steadily from 8,700 in 1993 to 32,500 in 1999 and

Table 4.1 China's Income Inequality across Time and Space

	Period	Gini coefficients		Income ratio of	
				Top 20%	Bottom 20%
		Initial year	Final year	Initial year	Final year
Nepal	1995–2003	37.65	47.30	6.19	9.47
China	1993–2004	40.74	47.25	7.57	11.37
India	1993–2004	32.89	36.22	4.85	5.52
Indonesia	1993–2002	34.37	34.30	5.20	5.13
Taipei, China	1993–2003	31.32	33.85	5.41	6.05
South Korea	1993–2004	28.68	31.55	4.38	5.47
Japan	1993	24.90		3.37	
Columbia	2003		58.60		25.30
Brazil	2004		56.99		23.00
Côte d'Ivoire	2002		44.60		9.70
Nigeria	2003		43.60		9.80
United States	2000		39.42		8.45
United Kingdom	2002		34.37		5.59

SOURCE: Asian Development Bank (2007) and United Nations (2006).

then to 74,000 in 2004. Second, the average number of persons in a mass incident has also risen greatly, from 8 in 1993 to 50 in 2004.[13] It should be noted, however, that these numbers might not accurately portray the degree that social unrest has increased because the data include disco brawls and gambling den raids as well as social protests (see East-SouthWestNorth [n.d.]).

Clearly, the number of mass incidents would have been lower if China had better governance. There would have been more preemptive efforts at conflict mediation by the government and less abuse of power if the government's actions had been monitored closely by an independent mechanism and if the government had also been held more accountable for its performance.

One main source of recent social unrest in rural China has been the conversion of farmland to industrial parks without adequate compensation to the farmers. It is interesting, therefore, that the No. 1 Document issued jointly in January 2006 by the CPC Central Committee and the State Council pledged not only to "stabilize and regulate the transfer of land-use rights and accelerate land acquisition reforms" but also to "expand channels to express public opinions in the countryside and improve the mechanism to resolve social conflicts" (Ma 2007b).[14]

The Hu-Wen leadership's desire to improve the institutions of governance is also borne out by the following report from the *South China Morning Post* (Xiangwei 2007) about what Premier Wen said when he met a group of Chinese citizens in Japan in April 2007:

> During 30 minutes of impromptu remarks, he said the key to pursuing social justice, the mainland's most important task, was to "let people be masters of their houses and make every cadre understand that power is invested in them by the people."
>
> . . . Although he did not deviate from the official line and spoke informally on both occasions, Mr. Wen is known for being careful about what he says, whether in prepared remarks or speaking off the cuff. The fact that he highlighted, in the presence of Hong Kong and overseas journalists, the need for political reform is uncharacteristic and interesting, particularly in the context of the leadership reshuffle looming at the Communist Party's 17th congress later this year.
>
> There have been signs that the leadership under President Hu Jintao is under increasing pressure to undertake drastic political reforms to consolidate the party's grip on power and stamp out widespread corruption.

While there are reasonable grounds for an analyst to doubt either the sincerity of Premier Wen's words or his ability to act on them, the analyst cannot doubt that Premier Wen is at least aware that democracy is one way to solve many of China's problems of governance. The embrace of the Harmonious Society program by the Hu-Wen leadership reveals CPC's acknowledgment that democracy, the rule of law, and a stable income distribution make up an indivisible combination that is necessary to ensure the social stability that will keep the economy on the high-growth path to catch up with the United States (a vision that acts as the bedrock of CPC's legitimacy to rule).

Power Supply Failure

China's emergence as a major trading nation has been accompanied by increasing conflicts with the European Union (EU) and the United States about China's trading practices and its exchange rate policy. The dissatisfaction over trade with China is evident from the following two press reports:

> Peter Mandelson, the EU trade commissioner . . . called various aspects of China's trade policy "illogical," "indefensible" and "unacceptable" and accused [China] of doing nothing to rein in rampant counterfeiting. . . . Mr. Mandelson also refused to grant China market economy status . . . [because it has] fulfilled [only] one of five criteria." (Bounds 2007)

> After years of inconclusive skirmishing, trade tensions between the United States and China are about to intensify. . . . "We are competing not only with a country with low wages but with very high and heavy subsidies and a rigging of their currency . . ." says Rep. Sander Levin, D-Mich., chairman of the House trade subcommittee. . . . "I hate the term trade war because it is always used when you try to get a fair break . . . ," he says: "Sometimes pressure works." (Lynch 2007)

While the trade deficit is many times identified as the cause of the trade tension, the true cause is the ongoing large shift in the international division of labor that has been set in motion by the post-1990 acceleration of globalization and by the continued fast pace of technological innovations. The next two sections argue that the trade tensions reflect, one, the pains of structural adjustment in the United States because of its very inadequate social safety nets, and, two, the dysfunctional nature of China's financial system.

CAUSES OF TRADE PROTECTIONISM AGAINST CHINA

Defects in the U.S. Economy

It is not uncommon to encounter allegations that the bilateral U.S.-China trade deficit represented the export of unemployment from China to the United States, and that it lowered the wage for labor. These allegations are not supported by the facts, however. Table 4.2 shows that the steady rise in the trade deficit from 1.2 percent of GDP in 1996 to 5.9 percent in 2006 was accompanied by a fall in the civilian unemployment rate from 5.4 percent in 1996 to 4.6 percent in 2006, and by a rise in the total compensation (measured in 2005 prices) received by a full-time worker from $48,175 in 1996 to $55,703 in 2005.[15]

What is fueling the resentment toward imports from China when the median U.S. worker is experiencing neither more unemployment nor lower compensation? The U.S. worker is feeling more insecure in the 2000s than in the 1980s because of faster turnover in employment. Globalization and technological innovations have required the worker to change jobs more often, and she finds that there are considerable costs associated with the job change because of the inadequacies in the U.S. social safety nets.

Table 4.2 documents the more frequent change in jobs by the declining trend in the length of the median job tenure for older male workers. The median job tenure for males in the

- 33–44 age group decreased from 7.0 years in 1987 to 5.1 years in 2006;

- 45–54 age group decreased from 11.8 years in 1987 to 8.1 years in 2006; and

- 55–64 age group decreased from 14.5 years in 1987 to 9.5 years in 2006.

In terms of social safety nets, Burtless (2005) reports that within the G-7 in 2004, only the United Kingdom has a less generous unemployment benefits scheme than the United States. An unemployed person in the United States received initial unemployment benefits that equaled 53 percent of previous income compared to 78 percent in Germany, 76 percent in Canada and France, 61 percent in Japan, 60 percent in Italy, and 46 percent in the United Kingdom. The duration of unemployment benefits was 6 months in the United States compared to 12 months in Germany, 9 months in Canada, 30 months in France, 10 months in Japan, and 6 months in Italy and the United Kingdom.

There are two major factors behind the more frequent changes in jobs. The first factor is globalization, especially the post-1990 integration of the labor force in the former Soviet Union, India, and China (SIC) into the international division of labor. Table 4.3 shows that the number of workers already engaged in the international division of labor in 1990 was 1,083 million, and the combined labor force of SIC was 1,232 million. The international division of labor in 1990 was certainly an unnatural one because half of the world's workforce had been kept out of it by the SIC's autarkic policies.

Table 4.2 Trade Balance, Unemployment Rate, Total Compensation for Labor, and Job Tenure in Selected Year

	1987	1996	2000	2006
Trade deficit as a percent of GDP	3.1	1.2	3.9	5.9
Unemployment rate (%)	6.2	5.4	4.0	4.6
Total compensation for a full-time equivalent employee (2005 $)	46,041	48,175	52,728	55,703[a]
Median tenure at job for male workers by age group (years)				
33–44	7.0	6.1	5.3	5.1
45–54	11.8	10.1	9.5	8.1
55–64	14.5	10.5	10.2	9.5

NOTES: Trade deficit and unemployment data are from the White House (2007). Data on compensation in real terms and 1987 data are from Burtless (2007). Data on average job tenure in 1996–2006 are from the Bureau of Labor Statistics: http://www.bls.gov/news.release/tenure.t01.htm.
[a] From 2005.

The economic isolation of the Soviet bloc started crumbling when the new noncommunist Solidarity government of Poland began the marketization and internationalization of the Polish economy on January 1, 1990.[16] For the Chinese elite, the end of the Soviet Union in August 1991 confirmed that there was no third way in the capitalism-versus-socialism debate. In early 1992, Deng Xiaoping entrenched China firmly on the path of convergence to a private market economy.[17] In 1991, India faced a balance of payments crisis, and it responded by going well beyond the administration of the standard corrective macroeconomic medicine of fiscal-monetary tightening and exchange rate devaluation into comprehensive adjustments of microeconomic incentives.

Table 4.3 Distribution of the Global Labor Force (millions)

	Global total	The non-SIC countries			The SIC countries			
		Non-SIC total	Developed economies	Developing economies	SIC total	China	India	Soviet bloc
1990	2,315	1,083	403	680	1,232	687	332	213
2000	2,672	1,289	438	851	1,383	764	405	214

SOURCE: Freeman (2004). Our figure for "Global total" in 2000 is different from that in Freeman.

A decade after the start of the deep integration of the SIC economies into the world economic system, the number of workers involved in the international economic system in 2000 had increased to 2,672 million (with 1,363 million workers from SIC); see Table 4.3. The Heckscher-Ohlin model would predict that this doubling of the world labor, achieved by bringing in cheaper labor from SIC, would lower the relative price of the labor-intensive good and hence reduce the real wage in the industrialized country.[18] Furthermore, the fact that U.S. capital could now move abroad to build production facilities in the SIC economies to service the U.S. market as well as third markets also gave globalization another channel to lower the U.S. wage.

However, the U.S. real wage has not fallen (Table 4.2). The reason is that the remarkably high U.S. productivity growth since the late 1980s (perhaps enabled in large part by the information and communications technology [ICT] revolution) prevented the real wage from declining. Furthermore, as the import competition is focused on the good that uses low-skilled labor intensively, the wage gap between low-skilled labor and high-skilled labor in the United States has widened. In short, the economic impact of globalization in the United States is therefore manifested in a diminished labor share of GDP, rather than in a lower real wage, and in an increased dispersion in U.S. wages.

While the Heckscher-Ohlin model does provide a coherent mechanism for globalization to have the above two wage outcomes, the inconvenient truth is that China might not be the most influential factor in these developments even though China accounted for 764 million of the combined SIC labor force of 1,383 million in 2000. China is unlikely to be the most important culprit because there are three other independent developments that have had important consequences for U.S. wages.

First, many technological innovations have substituted capital for labor and have transformed many of what have been traditionally nontradable services into tradable services, allowing jobs to be outsourced to foreign service providers. For example, the ICT revolution has allowed offshore call centers to handle questions from U.S. customers, offshore accountants to process U.S.-based transactions, and offshore medical technicians to read the X-rays of U.S. patients. The empirical literature suggests that technological innovations are likely to have had a bigger influence on U.S. wages than import competition from China.[19]

Second, institutional changes have attenuated labor share of income. Union membership has declined, reducing the bargaining power of labor. There has also been an upward shift in the compensation norms for high-level executives. Third, there has been increased immigration into the United States (before 2001), especially a disproportionate inward immigration of low-skilled labor.[20]

In short, much of the popular outcry in the United States and the European Union against China's trade surpluses is misplaced. A widening of the U.S. trade deficit creates additional stress on U.S. labor because U.S. imports are more labor-intensive than its exports. However, even if China's trade balance were zero, the pains of structural adjustment and income redistribution caused by technological innovations, institutional changes, globalization, and immigration would still be there; and the amount of worker anxiety they generated collectively would be much larger than the additional worker anxiety generated by the widening trade deficit.

If the United States strengthens its social safety nets to lower the cost of changing jobs, it could help reduce trade tensions between the United States and China. Specifically, the U.S. Congress should quicken the reduction in fiscal imbalance and expand trade adjustment programs, especially those that upgrade the skill of the younger workers. The Trade Adjustment Assistance (TAA) program still functions inadequately after its overhaul in 2002. Brainard (2007) reports that

> participation has remained surprisingly low, thanks in part to confusing Department of Labor interpretations and practices that ultimately deny benefits to roughly three-quarters of workers who are certified as eligible for them. TAA has helped fewer than 75,000 new workers per year, while denying more than 40 percent of all employers' petitions. And remarkably, the Department of Labor has interpreted the TAA statute as excluding the growing number of services workers displaced by trade. . . . Between 2001 and 2004, an average of only 64 percent of participants found jobs while they participated in TAA. And earnings on the new job were more than 20 percent below those prior to displacement.

The TAA program clearly needs further improvement. Brainard's (2007) proposal for the establishment of wage insurance is an excellent way to bring the U.S. social safety net more in line with the type of structural adjustments driven by globalization and technological changes.

DEFECTS IN THE CHINESE ECONOMY

China's chronic and growing overall trade surplus reveals a deep-seated serious problem in China's economy, its dysfunctional financial system. This problem is revealed by the aggregate-level accounting identity that the overall current account balance (of which, in China, the overall trade account is the biggest part) is determined by the fiscal position of the government, and the savings-investment decisions of the state-controlled enterprise (SCE) sector and the private sector, which together make up the nongovernment sector.[21] Specifically,

$$CA = (T - G) + (S_{SCE} - I_{SCE}) + (S_{private} - I_{private}),$$

where CA = current account in the balance of payments.

$CA = (X - M) + R$

X = export of goods and nonfactor services

M = import of goods and nonfactor services

R = net factor earnings from abroad (i.e., export of factor services)

T = state revenue

G = state expenditure (including state investment)

S_{SCE} = saving of the SCEs

I_{SCE} = investment of the SCEs

$S_{private}$ = saving of the private sector

$I_{private}$ = investment of the private sector

The Chinese fiscal position $(T - G)$ has for the last decade been a small deficit, so it is not the cause of the swelling current account surpluses in the 2000s. The current account surplus exists because the sum of savings by SCEs and the private sector exceeds the sum of their investment expenditures.

Why has China's financial system failed to translate the savings into investments? Such an outcome was not always the case. Before 1994, the voracious absorption of bank loans by SCEs to invest recklessly usually kept the current account negative and the creation of NPLs high.

When the government implemented stricter controls on the SOBs from 1994 onward (e.g., removing top bank officials whenever their bank lent more than its credit quota or allowed the NPL ratio to increase too rapidly), the SOBs slowed down the growth of loans to SCEs. This cutback created an excess of savings because the SOB-dominated financial sector did not then rechannel the released savings (which were also increasing) to finance the investment of the private sector. This failure in financial intermediation by the SOBs is quite understandable. First, the legal status of private enterprises was, until recently, lower than that of the state enterprises; and, second, there was no reliable way to assess the balance sheets of the private enterprises, which were naturally eager to escape taxation. The upshot was that the residual excess savings leaked abroad in the form of the current account surplus. Inadequate financial intermediation has made developing China a capital-exporting country.

This perverse current account outcome is not new. Taiwan had exactly this problem up to the mid-1980s, when all Taiwanese banks were state owned and operated according to the civil service regulation that required loan officers to repay any bad loans that they had approved. The result was a massive failure in financial intermediation that caused Taiwan's current account surplus to be 21 percent of GDP in 1986. The reason China has not been producing the gargantuan current account surpluses seen in Taiwan in the mid-1980s is because of the large amount of SCE investments.

Why is the nongovernment sector's savings rate rising? The combined savings of the SOE and non-SOE sectors rose from 20 percent in 1978 to 30 percent in 1987, and then went above 45 percent since 2004. In discussions about the increasing savings rate, a common view is that the rise reflects the uncertainty about the future that many SOE workers feel in the face of widespread privatization of loss-making SOEs. This explanation is incomplete because there also has been a rise in the rural savings rate, even though rural residents have little to fear about the loss of jobs in the state-enterprise sector because none of them are employed there.[22]

We see two general changes that have caused both urban and rural savings rates to rise significantly. The first is increased worries about the future. The steady decline in state subsidies to medical care, housing, loss-making enterprises, and education, along with mismanagement of pension funds by the state, have led people to save more to insure against future bad luck (e.g., sickness, job loss), buy their own homes, build up nest eggs for retirement, and invest in their children.

The second change is the secular improvement in the official Chinese attitude toward market capitalism. Given the high rate of return to capital, this increasingly business-friendly attitude of the Communist Party of China has encouraged both rural and urban residents to save for investment—that is, greater optimism about the future has spawned investment-motivated saving.[23]

In our explanations of the existence of the current account surpluses and the growth of the surplus, there is a common element in both—China's financial system. The fact is that savings behavior is not independent of the sophistication of the financial system. An advanced financial system will have a variety of financial institutions that would enable pooling of risks by providing medical insurance, pension insurance, and unemployment insurance, and transform savings into education loans, housing loans, and other types of investment loans to the private sector. Ceteris paribus, the more sophisticated a financial system, the lower the savings rate. China generates the current account surplus because of inadequate financial intermediation, and the surplus grows over time because the dysfunctional financial system fails to pool risks to reduce uncertainty-induced savings and fails to provide loans to reduce investment-motivated saving.

What is to be done in China? The obvious short-run policy package has two components. First, accelerate import liberalization (e.g., seriously implement the commitments made in negotiations for WTO membership, such as IPR protection) and expand beyond WTO specifications.

The second component of the short-run policy package is to have an expansionary fiscal policy (e.g., rural infrastructure investments) to soak up the excess savings, with an emphasis on import-intensive investments (e.g., buying airplanes and sending students abroad). It is important that time limits be put on the expanded public works and SCE investments because, in the long run, the increased public investments could follow an increasingly rent-seeking path that is wasteful (e.g., building a second big bridge to a lowly populated island to benefit a politically connected construction company, as in Japan), and the increased SCE investments could convert themselves into nonperforming loans at the SOBs.

Clearly, the optimum solution to the problem of excess saving is not for the government to absorb it by increasing its budget deficit but to establish an improved mechanism for coordinating private savings and private investments. The establishment of a modern financial system will not only achieve the objective of intermediating all of domestic saving into domestic investment; it will also enhance welfare and lower the savings rate by pooling risks through vehicles like medical insurance and pension insurance. In a nutshell, China's main challenge today is to develop smoothly functioning financial, planning, and regulatory systems that can employ the remaining rural surplus labor (as indicated by an average wage of about $120 per month for 480 million rural and migrant workers) and surplus capital, which now shows up as China's sustained current account surplus and rising foreign exchange reserves.

The important conclusion from this section is that U.S.-China trade tension would be lowered much more if both countries undertake corrective policies rather than if China acted alone, and that a wider range of policy instruments should be employed (e.g., wage insurance program in U.S. and financial market development in China) rather than relying just on exchange rate adjustment alone.

THE ENVIRONMENTAL COLLAPSE IN CHINA

The present mode of economic development has given China the dirtiest air in the world, is polluting more and more of the water resources, and is possibly changing the climate pattern within China.[24] The reality is that CPC's new objective of living in harmony with nature is not a choice because the Maoist adage of "man conquering nature" is just as unrealistic as creating prosperity through central planning. China's fast growth in the last two decades has done substantial damage to the environment. Economy (2004, pp. 18–19) summarizes the economic toll as follows:

> China has become home to six of the ten most polluted cities in the world. Acid rain now affects about one-third of China's territory, including approximately one-third of its farmland. More than 75 percent of the water in rivers flowing through China's urban areas is [unsuitable for human contact] . . . deforestation and grassland

degradation continue largely unabated. . . . The [annual] economic
cost of environmental degradation and pollution . . . are the equivalent of 8–12 percent of China's annual gross domestic product.

Water shortage appears to pose the most immediate environmental
threat to China's continued high growth. Presently, China uses 67–75
percent of the 800–900 billion cubic meters of water available annually, and present trends in water consumption project the usage rate
to be 78–100 percent in 2030 (Lee 2006). The present water situation
is actually already fairly critical because of the uneven distribution of
water and the lower than normal rainfall in the past 15 years. Right now,
"[about] 400 of China's 660 cities face water shortages, with 110 of
them severely short" (Noi 2004).[25]

The extended period of semidrought in northern China combined
with the economic and population growth have caused an increased
amount of water to be pumped from the aquifers, leading the water table
to drop three to six meters a year (Becker 2003; Ma 2003). And a study
using measurements from satellites (the Global Positioning System)
has established that the part of China north of the thirty-sixth parallel
latitude has been "sinking at the rate of 2 millimeters a year" (Becker
2003).[26] Specifically, "Shanghai, Tianjin, and Taiyuan are the worst hit
in China, with each sinking more than two meters (6.6 feet) since the
early 1990s" (Agence France-Presse 2004).

The overall water situation in northern China is reflected in the fate
of the Yellow River, "which started drying up every few years from
1972, did so for increasing periods of time over longer distances in
the 1990s until 1997, when it dried up for almost the entire year over a
stretch of several hundred kilometres" Noi (2004).

The utilization rate of Yellow River's water is 60 percent, far
exceeding the internationally recommended utilization limit of 40 percent. All the mentioned factors have contributed to lowering the "amount
of Yellow River water feeding into the Bohai Sea" from an annual 49.6
billion cubic meters in the 1960s to 14.2 billion cubic meters in the
1990s to the present 4.65 billion cubic meters (Lee 2006).

Water shortage and the increasing pollution of current water sup-
plies are not the only serious environmental threats to the economy of
northern China.[27] The desert is expanding (possibly at an accelerating
pace), and human activities appear to be the chief culprit. The State For-
estry Administration reported that 28 percent of the country's land mass

was affected by desertification in 1999, and 37 percent was affected by soil erosion. The report identified about 65 percent of the desert as having been created by "overcultivation, overgrazing, deforestation, and poor irrigation practices" (*South China Morning Post* 2002). The rate of desertification is 3,900 square miles a year, an annual loss of a land area twice the size of Delaware.[28] One direct upshot is a great increase in the frequency of major sandstorms, which plays "havoc with aviation in northern China for weeks, cripples high-tech manufacturing and worsens respiratory problems as far downstream as Japan, the Korean peninsula and even the western United States" (French 2004).[29] In the assessment of Chen Lai, vice minister of water resources, "It will take nearly half a century for China to control the eroded land and rehabilitate their damaged ecosystems in accordance with China's present erosion-control capabilities" (*South China Morning Post* 2002).

While northern China has been getting drier and experiencing desertification, nature, as if in compensation (or in mockery), has been blasting southern China with heavier rains, causing heavy floods that have brought considerable deaths and property damage almost every summer since 1998.[30] The sad possibility is that the northern droughts and southern floods may not be independent events but a combination caused by pollution that originates in China. I will have more to say about this possibility later.

Clearly, without water, growth cannot endure. And in response, the government began implementation in 2002 of Mao Zedong's 1952 proposal that three canals—each over 1,000 miles long—be built to bring water from the south to the north: 1) an eastern coastal canal from Jiangsu to Shandong and Tianjin, 2) a central canal from Hubei to Beijing and Tianjin, and 3) a western route from Tibet to the northwestern provinces (Phan 2002). Construction of the eastern canal (which would be built on a part of the existing Grand Canal) started in 2002, and the central canal in 2003. Work on the western canal was scheduled to begin in 2010 upon completion of the first stage of the central canal.

The scale of this water transfer project is simply unprecedented anywhere: "Together, the three channels would pump about 48 billion liters of water a year—enough to fill New York's taps for a quarter century. Only a tenth as much water flows through the next-largest water diversion project, in California" (Phan 2002).

This massive construction project will not only be technically challenging but also extremely sensitive politically and fraught with environmental risks. The central canal will have to tunnel through the foot of the huge dyke that contains the elevated Yellow River, and the western canal will have to transport water through regions susceptible to freezing. The number of people displaced by the Three Gorges Dam was 1.1 million, and this water transfer scheme is a bigger project. The enlargement of the Danjiangkou Dam (in Hubei) alone to enable it to be the source of the central canal will already displace 330,000 people (Cheung 2003).[31] Moving people involuntarily is certainly potentially explosive politically. The project could also be politically explosive on the international front as well. One plan for the western canal calls for "damming the Brahmaputra river and diverting 200 billion cubic metres of water annually to feed the ageing Yellow River," a scenario that is reportedly "giving sleepless nights to the Indian government . . . [which is concerned that this Great Western Water Diverson Project] could have immense impact on lower riparian states like India and Bangladesh" (Bagchi 2006).

The potential environmental damages caused by this project are the most serious for the central and western canals. In the case of the central canal,

> environmental experts [in Wuhan where the Hanjiang River flows into the Yangtze] are worried about . . . [whether the annual extraction of 8 billion cubic meters of water could affect] the river's ability to flush out the massive pollution flows released by the thousands of factories and industries along the tributaries. . . . The reduced flows could increase the frequency of toxic red algae blooms on the Yangtze near the confluence with the Hanjiang River. There have already been three blooms . . . [by May of that year, 2003]. (Cheung 2003)

The western canal has generated a lively controversy. Some scientists are contending that it "would cause more ecological damage than good" (Oster 2006b) because it "could cause dramatic climate changes . . . [and] the changed flow and water temperature would lead to a rapid decline in fish and other aquatic species" (Simons 2006).

Many opponents of the water transfer project have argued that water conservation could go a long way toward addressing this problem because currently a tremendous amount of the water is wasted—only

50 percent of China's industrial water is recycled compared to 80 percent in the industrialized countries Noi (2004), and China consumes 3,860 cubic meters of water to produce $10,000 of GDP compared to the world average of 965 cubic meters (*Straits Times* 2004). The most important reason for this inefficient use of water lies in the fact that "China's farmers, factories and householders enjoy some of the cheapest water in the world" (Holland 2006), even though China's per capita endowment of water is a quarter of the world average (*Straits Times* 2004).

There is, however, the unhappy possibility that neither the price mechanism nor the three canals can solve China's water problem and make its growth sustainable unless the present mode of economic development is drastically amended. There is now persuasive evidence that China's voluminous emission of black carbon (particles of incompletely combusted carbon) has contributed significantly to a shift in the climate pattern that produces northern droughts and southern floods of increasing intensity (Menon et al. 2002; Streets 2005). The biggest source of what has been called the "Asian brown cloud" in the popular media is burning of coal and bio-fuels in China. If the pollution-induced climate change analysis is valid, it means that

- China's massive reforestation program will not succeed in reducing sandstorms in the north because trees cannot survive if the amount of rainfall is declining over time;
- the number of south-north canals will have to be increased over time to meet the demand for water in northern China; and
- China needs to significantly reduce its emission of black carbon (presuming no new large emissions from neighboring countries like India).

The general point is that effective policy making on the environmental front is a very difficult task because much of the science about the problem is not known. For example, China must no longer separate its water and energy strategies. A systems approach in policy making is necessary because the interaction among the outcomes from the different sectoral policies can generate serious unintended environmental damage. If part of the shift in China's climate is integral to global climate change, then a sustainable development policy would require a complete rethinking about the location of population centers and types of enhanced international cooperation on global environmental management.

The uncomfortable reality for China is that unless ecological balance is restored within the medium term, environmental limits could choke off further economic growth. And the uncomfortable reality for the rest of the world is that the negative consequences of large-scale environmental damage within a geographically large country are seldom confined within that country's borders. The continued march of China's desertification first brought more frequent sandstorms to Beijing and has sent yellow dust clouds not only across the sea to neighboring Japan and Korea but also across the ocean to the United States. China's environmental management is a concern not only for China's welfare but for global welfare as well.

In discussing the environmental aspects of the water transfer plan, it is important to note that there is now an open controversy in China involving a key government infrastructure project, and that this controversy is not limited to members of the technocracy. The very public nature of the controversy and the involvement of more than just scientists, engineers, and economists in it reveal how very far social attitudes have progressed. The important point is that this change in social expectations will require any government in China to live in harmony with nature. However, any government will have great difficulties in doing so even if it wants to, because a green growth policy involves a systems approach, and scientific understanding of many ecological subsystems and the nature of their interactions is still rather incomplete.

Proper management of the environment has now become critical for China if it is to continue its industrialization process. The unexpurgated version of a 2007 World Bank reported that "about 750,000 people die prematurely in China each year, mainly from air pollution in large cities" (McGregor 2007), and a 2007 OECD study estimates that "China's air pollution will cause 20 million people a year to fall ill with respiratory diseases" (Anderlini 2007). Pan Yue, the deputy head of the State Environmental Protection Agency, summed up the present situation in China very well when he said, "If we continue on this path of traditional industrial civilization, there is no chance that we will have sustainable development. China's population, resources, and environment have already reached the limits of their capacity to cope. Sustainable development and new sources of energy are the only road that we can take" (Kynge 2004).

CONCLUSION

In appraising whether the attainment of the October 2006 vision of a Harmonious Society would be sufficient to sustain high economic growth in China, the greatest inadequacy I see is the absence of a parallel objective to build a harmonious world. A harmonious society cannot endure in China unless there is also a harmonious world, and vice versa. China's pursuit of such a society requires it to actively help provide two global public goods that make a harmonious world possible: the strengthening of the multilateral free trade system and the protection of the global environmental commons.

China has benefited immensely from the GATT-WTO free-trade regime, and yet up to this point it has played a passive role in pushing the Doha Round negotiations forward to completion. By default, Brazil and India have assumed the leadership of the developing economies camp in the trade negotiations. According to Susan Schwab, the U.S. Trade Representative, at the G4 (United States, European Union, Brazil, and India) meeting in Potsdam in June 2007, Brazil and India retreated from their earlier offers to reduce their manufacturing tariffs in return for cuts in agricultural subsidies by the developed economies because of "their fear of growing Chinese imports" (Beattie, Callan, and Pilling 2007; Luce and Callan 2007). The Brazilian-Indian action caused the Potsdam talks to fail and hurt the many developing economies that were agricultural exporters.

China should now seek a leadership role in the Doha Round negotiations that is commensurate with its participation in international trade. Failure of the Doha Round could set in motion the unraveling of multilateral free trade because the present international atmosphere is right for protectionism. The United States, which has traditionally been a leader in expanding the multilateral free trade system, is now beset by self-doubt for three major reasons.

First, the United States was willing to endure the pains of structural adjustments in the 1960–1990 period to accommodate the growing imports from Japan, South Korea, Taiwan, and ASEAN because they were frontline allies in the Cold War. When the Cold War ended, it was natural for the United States to reconsider the economic cost of structural adjustment because the security and ideological benefits from it went down.

Second, the amount of required structural adjustment in the United States to accommodate the rise of the SIC bloc is far greater than the earlier adjustment to the rise of its Cold War allies. As noted, the entry of the former SIC economies has doubled the labor force participating in the international division of labor.

Third, the strongest lobby for free trade in the United States has been the economics profession, and the free trade doctrine has come under strong internal criticism in the last few years. Paul Samuelson has made many fundamental contributions to the development of the standard trade models that convinced mainstream economists that free trade is the best policy, and it was therefore an intellectual earthquake when he argued in 2004 that under free trade, where outsourcing accelerates the transfer of knowledge to the developing country, there could be a decline in the welfare of the developed country (see Bernstein [2004] and Samuelson [2004]).

While the veracity of the Samuelson hypothesis is uncertain, the hypothesis clearly reflects the widespread pains of structural adjustment that they witness around them—a phenomenon captured by the decreasing length of median job tenure. In April 2007, the United States bypassed multilateralism in free trade by agreeing to form a Free Trade Area with South Korea. With the United States weakening in its resolve to protect the multilateral free trade system, China should now become more active in the Doha Round negotiations to further deregulate world trade. Such a role will be very much in China's interest because Brazil is now bypassing multilateral trade liberalization by entering into Free Trade Area negotiations with the European Union. The fact is that a growing number of nations like Brazil "are increasingly wary of a multilateral deal because it would mandate tariff cuts, exposing them more deeply to low-cost competition from China. Instead, they are seeking bilateral deals with rich countries that are tailored to the two parties' needs" (Miller 2007). It is time for China to show that it is a responsible stakeholder by joining in the stewardship of the multilateral free trade system.

The global environment is the second area where China can help to build a harmonious world system. Specifically, China should be mobilizing international consensus to form an international research consortium to develop ways to burn coal cleanly because China is now building a power station a week and is hence able to facilitate extensive experimentation on prototype plants to burn coal cleanly. If successful, this global cooperation on clean energy research will unleash sustainable development in China as well as the rest of the world.

We realize, of course, that while the need to maintain high growth could motivate China to become more active in supplying global public goods, it might not be allowed to do so because of the usual reluctance of the existing dominant powers to share the commanding heights of the world political leadership. The sad experience of Japan being denied permanent membership in the Security Council of the United Nations is a case in point. Harmonious international relations are the omitted item in China's perception of a Harmonious Society in 2006, and it could turn out to be a very soft spot in the Chinese growth engine.

Besides the adept management of international relations, the competent management of economic issues is also fundamental to maintaining China's path to high growth. The most important realization on this front is that in today's China, doing more of the same economic policies will not produce the same salubrious results on every front because the development problems have changed. For example, in the first phase of economic development, the provision of more jobs (through economic deregulation) was enough to lower poverty significantly. Many of the people who are still poor require more than just job opportunities; they need an infusion of assistance (e.g., empower them with human capital through education and health interventions) in order to take advantage of these job opportunities.

On the fiscal management front, my analysis suggests that the management of state assets and the regulation of the financial sector should be reformed to eliminate the phenomenon of repeated recapitalization of the SOBs. The privatization of some units of the SOBs, and the emergence of large domestic private banks will help strengthen the budget constraints perceived by the managers of SOBs.

The fact is, however, that the probability of a software failure and the probability of a power supply failure are both higher than the probability of a hardware failure. This means that development policy making in China has become more challenging. There must now not only be more adroit but also fuller accommodation of domestic social demands in order to keep China's growth rate high. The reality is that popular satisfaction with the status quo depends inversely on the level of expectations, and the expectations of the Chinese people toward their government have risen dramatically along with income and, more importantly, along with their growing knowledge of the outside world. A Chinese government that consistently fails to produce results in line with the rise in social expectations runs the increasing risk of being challenged by another faction within the CPC, culminating in an open split with each side seeking the support of nonparty groups.

Complicating matters is that there has not only been rising expectations but also diversification of expectations. In this new situation, the greater use of democratic procedures, the establishment of an independent judiciary, and the restoration of a free press might be inevitable if CPC is to successfully accommodate the rising social expectations and mediate the emerging differences in social expectations. What will happen will depend on whether the CPC is sufficiently confident that it will be politically skillful enough to lead the democratic transition and emerge afterward as the most important political force. History tells us that the French and British monarchies reacted very differently to the popular requests for reform, and the outcomes were very different in each case.

Notes

I was deeply honored to deliver this paper as the Werner Sichel Lecture at Western Michigan University on October 7, 2016. I am extremely grateful for the guidance I received in the discussion for revising the lecture. The insightful comments of Professor Huizhong Zhou and Professor Wei-Chiao Huang were most helpful.

1. Lardy (1998) wrote that "China's major banks are even weaker than most official data suggest. . . . On a realistic accounting, these banks' capital adequacy is negative, and they are insolvent (p. 95). . . . The failure of China's largest financial institutions would disrupt the flow of credit and disrupt the payments system, leading to a collapse of economic activity. The failure of major banks also could have long-term implications for the household savings rate. . . . A lower savings rate would mean a lower rate of investment and slower growth, in turn depressing the rate of new job creation, leading to sustained higher levels of unemployment" (pp. 143–144).

2. According to Pei (2006), "In a 'trapped transition,' the ruling elites have little interest in real reforms. They may pledge reforms, but most such pledges are lip service or tactical adjustments aimed at maintaining the status quo."

3. As Huang (2006) sees that India does not discriminate against its indigenous capitalists in favor of foreign capitalists, he predicts that "[u]nless China embarks on bold institutional reforms, India may very well outperform it in the next 20 years."

4. For a review of the debate on how to interpret China's high growth in the 1978–2000 and why China, unlike the economies of the former Soviet bloc, did not experience a recession when it made the switch from a centrally planned economy to a market economy, see Sachs and Woo (2000) and Woo (2001).

5. For example, President Soeharto of Indonesia was pushed out of office in May 1998, one month after raising fuel prices.

6. f has been above 1.5 percent for the past seven years; r was 4 percent in the past only because the interest rate was regulated. I think that the implementation of financial deregulation that is necessary for normal healthy development of the financial sector will render r to be at least 6 percent because 1) according to Solow (1991), the stylized fact for the real interest rate in the United States is that it is 5–6 percent; and 2) both the marginal rate of return to capital and the black market loan rate have been more than 20 percent.

7. The asymmetry is from the absence of financial punishment when a loss occurs.

8. Lipton and Barboza (2007) also report the recall of a ghoulish fake eyeball that was filled with kerosene, and of an infant wrist rattle that was a choking hazard.

9. For example, radial tires were manufactured without the gum strips that prevented the tires from separating; see Martin (2007).

10. This point was made by the popular tabloid *Southern Metropolis Daily*; see Buckley (2007).

11. This point was made by the Shanxi governor, Yu Youjun, who said, "For a long time, relevant government departments did little to regulate rural workshops, small coal mines and small factories, and they are basically out of control and are not being supervised. . . . The dereliction of duty by civil servants and the corruption of individuals have made it possible for illegal labour to exist, particularly the abductions of migrant workers, and forced labour of children and mentally disabled people" (Ma 2007a).

12. The Gini coefficient has a value between 0 and 1, and the higher the value, the greater the degree of income inequality.

13. The 1993 number is from Keidel (2006, p. 1), and the 2004 number is from Pei (2005), who wrote that, in 2004, there were 74,000 "mass incidents" involving 3.7 million people compared to 10,000 such incidents involving 730,000 people in 1994. Possibly, because of the widespread attention in the Western media on the marked rise in mass incidents, the post-2004 definition of mass incidents appeared to have been changed, making post-2004 data not comparable with the 1994–2004 data; see discussion in EastSouthWestNorth (n.d.).

14. The No. 1 Document designation shows that this is the most important task in the new year.

15. This positive wage trend for the average worker is also seen in that for the average blue-collar worker; see Woo (2008).

16. The economic transition and political disintegration of the Soviet bloc became irreversible when Yeltsin replaced Gorbachev as the unambiguous leader of Russia in August 1991 and implemented market-oriented reforms in January 1992.

17. Today, under the heading of a socialist market economy with Chinese characteristics, the Chinese constitution gives private property the same legal status as public property, and the Chinese Communist Party accepts capitalists as members.

18. More accurately, the wage of the formerly isolated SIC worker would rise while the wage for the worker in the industrialized country would fall.

19. There is a large empirical literature on the relative impact of technological changes and globalization on the U.S. wage rate; see for example, Sachs and Shatz (1994) and Feenstra and Hanson (1996).

20. Ottaviano and Peri (2005) offer a good discussion of this topic.

21. The SCE category covers companies, which are classified as SOBs, and joint-venture and joint-stock companies, which are controlled by third parties (e.g., legal persons).

22. Economist Intelligence Unit (2004, p. 23) reported that "farmers' propensity to save seems to have increased."

23. Liu and Woo (1994) and Woo and Liu (1995) contain formal modeling and econometric support for the investment-motivated saving hypothesis.

24. Air pollution is a serious problem. Of the 20 cities in the world identified by the World Bank as having the dirtiest air, 16 of them are in China. It is shocking that lead and mercury poisoning are more common than expected. See *Financial Times* (2004) and Oster (2006a).

25. The shortage is reported to be most acute in Taiyuan in Shanxi and Tianjin (Becker 2003).

26. Some 60 percent of the land in Tianjin municipality is plagued by subsistence (Becker 2003).

27. Examples of serious water pollution are Agence France-Presse (2006); Ma (2001); *Straits Times* (2003); Yardley (2004, 2006).

28. This is average of the 3,800 square miles reported in Howard (2004) and the 4,014 square miles reported in the *South China Morning Post* (2002).

29. The number of major sandstorms in China was 5 in the 1950–1959 period, 8 in 1960–1969, 13 in 1970–1979, 14 in 1980–1989, 23 in 1990–1999, 14 in 2000, 26 in 2001, 16 in 2002, and 11 in 2003, according to Pumin (2005).

30. The National Development and Reform Commission (2007) reported: "The regional distribution of precipitation shows that the decrease in annual precipitation was significant in most of northern China, eastern part of the northwest, and northeastern China, averaging 20~40 mm/10a, with decrease in northern China being most severe; while precipitation significantly increased in southern China and southwestern China, averaging 20~60 mm/10a. . . . The frequency and intensity of extreme climate/weather events throughout China have experienced obvious changes during the last 50 years. Drought in northern and northeastern China,

and flood in the middle and lower reaches of the Yangtze River and southeastern China have become more severe."

31. A lower estimate of 300,000 is given in Eckholm (2002).

References

Agence France-Presse. 2004. "Chinese Cities, including Olympic Host Beijing, Slowly Sinking." July 23.

———. 2006. "'Cancer Villages' Pay Heavy Price for Economic Progress." *South China Morning Post*, May 8.

Anderlini, Jamil. 2007. "OECD Highlights Chinese Pollution." *Financial Times*, July 17.

Asian Development Bank. 2007. "Key Indicators: Inequality in Asia." In *Key Indicators 2007*. Vol. 2. Manila: Asian Development Bank. https://www.adb.org/sites/default/files/publication/27729/key-indicators-2007.pdf (accessed June 2, 2017).

Bagchi, Indrani. 2006. "China's River Plan Worries India." *Times of India*, October 23.

Barboza, David. 2007a. "2nd Ingredient Is Suspected in Pet Food Contamination." *New York Times*, May 9, C:3.

———. 2007b. "A Slippery, Writhing Trade Dispute." *New York Times*, July 3, C:1.

———. 2007c. "When Fakery Turns Fatal." *New York Times*, June 5, C:1.

———. 2007d. "Ex-Chief of China Food and Drug Unit Sentenced to Death for Graft." *New York Times*, May 30, A:7.

Barboza, David, and Alexei Barrionuevo. 2007. "In China, Additive in Animals' Food Is an Open Secret." *New York Times*, April 1, A:1.

Barboza, David, and Walt Bogdanich. 2007. "China Questions 2 Companies in Contaminated Toothpaste Exports." *New York Times*, May 22, C:1.

Barboza, David, and Louise Story. 2007. "Train Wreck." *New York Times*, June 19, C:1.

Beattie, Alan, Eoin Callan, and David Pilling. 2007. "China's Shadow Looms over Doha Failure." *Financial Times*, June 23, p. 5.

Becker, Jasper. 2003. "Northern China Sinking . . . as the South Rises." *Straits Times*, March 18.

Bernstein, Aaron. 2004. "Shaking Up Trade Theory." *Bloomberg Businessweek*, December 6, p. 118.

Bogdanich, Walt. 2007. "China Prohibits Industrial Solvent in Toothpaste." *New York Times*, July 12, C:4.

Bogdanich, Walt, and Jake Hooker. 2007. "From China to Panama, a Trail of Poisoned Medicine." *New York Times*, May 6, A:1.

Bounds, Andrew. 2007. "Surplus Fuels EU-China War of Words." *Financial Times*, June 12.

Brainard, Lael. 2007. Testimony on Meeting the Challenge of Income Instability, Joint Economic Committee Hearing, February 28, 2007, Washington, DC.

Buckley, Chris. 2007. "China Slave Scandal Brings Resignation Calls." *Reuters*, June 18.

Burtless, Gary. 2005. "Income Supports for Workers and Their Families: Earnings Supplements and Health Insurance." Paper presented at the Workforce Policies for the Next Decade and Beyond conference held in Washington, DC, November 11.

———. 2007. "Income Progress across the American Income Distribution, 2000–2005." Testimony for the Committee on Finance, U.S. Senate, May 10, 2007, Washington, DC.

Chang, Gordon G. 2001. *The Coming Collapse of China*. New York: Random House.

Cheung, Ray. 2003. "Massive Scheme Aims to Quench China's Thirst." *South China Morning Post*, May 12.

China Daily. 2005. "Income Gap in China Widens in First Quarter." *China Daily*, June 19.

———. 2007. "China to Investigate into 'Slave Labor' Incident." *China Daily*, June 16.

Démurger, Sylvie, Jeffrey D. Sachs, Wing Thye Woo, Shuming Bao, Gene Chang, and Andrew Mellinger. 2002. "Geography, Economic Policy, and Regional Development in China." *Asian Economic Papers* 1(1): 146–197.

EastSouthWestNorth. N.d. "Statistics of Mass Incidents." EastSouthWestNorth (blog). http://zonaeuropa.com/20061115_1.htm (accessed June 2, 2017).

Eckholm, Erik. 2002. "China Will Move Water to Quench Thirst of Cities." *New York Times*, August 27, A:1.

Economist Intelligence Unit. 2004. "Country Report: China." London: *Economist*.

Economy, Elizabeth C. 2004. *The River Runs Black: The Environmental Challenge to China's Future*. Ithaca, NY: Cornell University Press.

Feenstra, Robert C., and Gordon H. Hanson. 1996. "Globalization, Outsourcing, and Wage Inequality." *American Economic Review* 86(2): 240–245.

Financial Times. 2004. "China's Economic Miracle Contains Mercuric Threat," December 18.

———. 2007. "Fisher-Price Recalls 1.5m China-Made Toys." *Financial Times*, August 2.

Freeman, Richard. 2004. "Doubling the Global Work Force: The Challenge of Integrating China, India, and the Former Soviet Bloc into the World Economy." Unpublished manuscript. Cambridge, MA: Harvard University.

French, Howard W. 2004. "Billions of Trees Planted, and Nary a Dent in the Desert." *New York Times*, April 11.

———. 2007. "Reports of Forced Labor at Brick Kilns Unsettle China." *New York Times*, June 16, A:3.

Holland, Tom. 2006. "Water Wastage Will Soon Leave China High and Dry." *South China Morning Post*, March 8.

Huang, Yasheng. 2006. "China Could Learn from India's Slow and Quiet Rise." *Financial Times*, January 23.

———. 2008. *Capitalism with Chinese Characteristics: Entrepreneurship and the State*. New York: Cambridge University Press.

Keidel, Albert. 2006. "China's Social Unrest: The Story behind the Stories." Policy Brief No. 48. Washington, DC: Carnegie Endowment for International Peace.

Kynge, James. 2004. "Modern China Is Facing an Ecological Crisis." *Financial Times*, July 26.

Lardy, Nicholas R. 1998. *China's Unfinished Economic Revolution*. Washington, DC: Brookings Institution.

Lee, Georgina. 2006. "Top Official Warns of Looming Water Crisis." *South China Morning Post*, November 7.

Lipton, Eric S., and David Barboza. 2007. "As More Toys Are Recalled, the Trail Ends in China." *New York Times*, June 19, A:1.

Liu, Liang-Yn, and Wing Thye Woo. 1994. "Saving Behavior under Imperfect Financial Markets and the Current Account Consequences." *Economic Journal* 104(424): 512–527.

Luce, Edward, and Eoin Callan. 2007. "Schwab Surprised by Stance of India and Brazil." *Financial Times*, June 22.

Lynch, David J. 2007. "Tensions Push Congress to Get Even with China." *USA Today*, June 13, A:1.

Ma, Josephine. 2003. "Main Rivers Facing a Pollution Crisis." *South China Morning Post*, June 6.

———. 2007a. "Fears Linger over Child Slaves at Kilns." *South China Morning Post*, June 23.

———. 2007b. "New Pledge to Give Farmers a Louder Voice." *South China Morning Post*, January 30.

Ma, Michael. 2001. "Northern Cities Sinking as Water Table Falls." *South China Morning Post*, August 11.

Martin, Andrew. 2007a. "F.D.A. Curbs Sale of 5 Seafoods Farmed in China." *New York Times*, June 29, A:1.

————. 2007b. "Chinese Tires Are Ordered Recalled." *New York Times*, June 26, C:1.

McGregor, Richard. 2007. "750,000 a Year Killed by Chinese Pollution." *Financial Times*, July 2.

McKibbin Warwick J., and Wing Thye Woo. 2003. "The Consequences of China's WTO Accession on Its Neighbours." *Asian Economic Papers* 2(2): 1–38.

Menon, Surabi, James Hansen, Larissa Nazarenko, and Yunfeng Luo. 2002. "Climate Effects of Black Carbon in China and India." *Science* 297: 2250–2253.

Miller, John W. 2007. "Brazil, Others Push Outside Doha for Trade Pacts." *Wall Street Journal*, July 5, A:6.

National Development and Reform Commission. 2007. "China's National Climate Change Programme." Beijing: NDRC. http://en.ndrc.gov.cn/newsrelease/200706/P020070604561191006823.pdf (accessed June 5, 2017).

New York Times. 2007. "5 Chinese Arrested in Enslavement Case." *New York Times*, June 18.

Noi, Goh Sui. 2004. "China May Be Left High and Dry." *Straits Times*, January 3.

O'Connor, James. 1973. *The Fiscal Crisis of the State*. New York: St. Martin's Press.

O'Neill, Jim, Dominic Wilson, Roopa Purushothaman, and Anna Stupnytska. 2005. "How Solid Are the BRICs?" Global Economics Paper No. 134. New York: Goldman Sachs.

Organisation for Economic Co-operation and Development (OECD). 2006. *Challenges for China's Public Spending: Toward Greater Effectiveness and Equity*. Paris: Organisation for Economic Co-Operation and Development.

Oster, Shai. 2006a. "A Poison Spreads amid China's Boom." *Wall Street Journal*, September 30, A:1.

————. 2006b. "China Water Plan Sows Discord." *Wall Street Journal*, October 20.

Ottaviano, Gianmarco I. P., and Giovanni Peri. 2005. "Rethinking the Gains from Immigration: Theory and Evidence from the U.S." NBER Working Paper No. 11672. Cambridge, MA: National Bureau of Economic Research.

Pei, Minxin. 2005. "China Is Paying the Price of Rising Social Unrest." *Financial Times*, November 7.

————. 2006. "China Is Stagnating in Its 'Trapped Transition'." *Financial Times*, February 24.

Phan, Anh-thu. 2002. "Ambitious Canal Network Aims to Meet Growing Demands." *South China Morning Post*, November 27.

Pumin, Yin. 2005. "Sands of Time Running Out: Desertification Continues to Swallow up 'Healthy' Land at an Alarming Rate." *Beijing Review*, June 16.

Reuters. 2007. "China Brickwork Slave Children May Number 1,000." Reuters, June 15.

Sachs, Jeffrey D., and Howard J. Shatz. 1994. "Trade and Jobs in U.S. Manufacturing." *Brookings Papers on Economic Activity* 1: 1–84.

Sachs, Jeffrey D., and Wing Thye Woo. 2000. "Understanding China's Economic Performance," *Journal of Policy Reform* 4(1): 1–50.

Samuelson, Paul. 2004. "Where Ricardo and Mill Rebut and Confirm Arguments of Mainstream Economists Supporting Globalization." *Journal of Economic Perspectives* 18(3): 135–146.

Simons, Craig. 2006. "Chinese Water Plan Opens Rift between Science, Art." *Austin American-Statesman*, September 10, A:15.

Solow, Robert. 1991. "Sustainability: An Economist's Perspective." In *Economics of the Environment: Selected Readings*, Robert N. Stavins, ed., 4th ed. The 18th J. Seward Johnson Lecture to the Marine Policy Center, Woods Hole Oceanographic Institution. New York: W.W. Norton, pp. 131–138.

South China Morning Post. 2002. "China Approves Project to Divert Water to Arid North." November 26.

Straits Times. 2004. "Alert Sounded over Looming Water Shortage." June 10.

Streets, David. 2005. "Black Smoke in China and Its Climate Effects." *Asian Economic Papers* 4(2): 1–23.

United Nations. 2006. *2006 Human Development Report.* New York: United Nations.

Woo, Wing Thye. 2001. "Recent Claims of China's Economic Exceptionalism: Reflections Inspired by WTO Accession." *China Economic Review* 12(2/3): 107–136.

———. 2008. "Understanding the Sources of Friction in U.S.-China Trade Relations: The Exchange Rate Debate Diverts Attention away from Optimum Adjustment." *Asian Economic Papers* 7(3): 65–99.

Woo, Wing Thye, Wen Hai, Yibiao Jin, and Gang Fan. 1994. "How Successful Has Chinese Enterprise Reform Been? Pitfalls in Opposite Biases and Focus." *Journal of Comparative Economics* 18(3): 410–437.

Woo, Wing Thye, Shi Li, Ximing Yue, Harry Xiaoying Wu, and Xinpeng Xu. 2004. *The Poverty Challenge for China in the New Millennium.* Report to the Poverty Reduction Taskforce of the Millennium Development Goals Project of the United Nations. New York: United Nations.

Woo, Wing Thye, and Liang-Yn Liu. 1995. "Investment-Motivated Saving and Current Account Malaise." *Asia-Pacific Economic Review* 1(2): 55–68.

World Bank. 2001. *China: Overcoming Rural Poverty.* Washington, DC: World Bank.

Xiangwei, Wang. 2007. "Impromptu Remarks Reveal the Party's Pressure for Reforms." *South China Morning Report*, April 16.

Yardley, Jim. 2004. "Rivers Run Black, and Chinese Die of Cancer." *New York Times*, September 12.

———. 2006. "Rules Ignored, Toxic Sludge Sinks Chinese Village." *New York Times*, September 4, A:1.

Zhouqiong, Wang. 2007. "More Forced into Prostitution, Labor." *China Daily*, July 27, 1.

5

State Enterprise Reform in China

Grasp or Release?

Mary E. Lovely
Yang Liang
Syracuse University

Beginning in the mid-1990s, the Chinese government moved aggressively to close loss-making state-owned enterprises (SOEs) and to restructure underperforming state assets deemed central to economic development. Over the next decade, the state laid off almost 50 million workers—40 percent of the public-enterprise workforce (Naughton 2007, p. 179). The adjustment of labor and other factors to this restructuring accommodated the rise of private enterprises and ushered in a sustained period of productivity growth. The wealth of newly minted entrepreneurs attested to the success of China's "privatization" of its industrial sector (Lardy 2014; Nee and Opper 2012).

While much attention has focused on the performance of China's private sector, its state sector is now coming under renewed international scrutiny. Even with the ascendancy of the private sector, China's state-owned and state-controlled enterprises have hardly disappeared and are among the country's largest firms. Geopolitically, this renewed interest is partly due to trade conflict in industries dominated by state enterprises, such as steel and shipbuilding, where shifts in global demand following the Great Recession led to global overcapacity and falling prices. Despite two decades of reform, state enterprises continue to dominate major sectors of the Chinese economy and have also emerged as global titans. Kowalski et al. (2013) investigate the extent of state ownership among the world's 2,000 largest companies—the so-called Forbes Global 2,000—and their 330,000 subsidiaries worldwide. Using an equally weighted average of shares of state-owned enterprises in sales, assets, and market value of the country's top 10 firms, they find that China tops the list of countries with the highest state presence among its globally elite enterprises.

That state firms remain an important aspect of the Chinese economy is not a surprise since, as Naughton (2007) notes, "there has never been a clearly articulated rationale for privatization" (p. 324). Without a specific privatization policy, the nature of industrial restructuring must be discerned from the historical record. In this chapter, we examine the characteristics of firms that were retained by the Chinese state and those that were released to the private sector. We begin our analysis by tracking the evolution of enterprises away from China's state sector, a task complicated by alternative definitions of state control, limited data, and opaque ownership arrangements. An initial contribution of this chapter, then, is the provision of new estimates of the size of the state sector, with a comparison to other recent characterizations in the literature.

To better understand the factors that influenced state decision making, we review and categorize various descriptions of the objectives of both central and local governments in enterprise restructuring. We then formulate these views as hypotheses and test them using data from China's Annual Survey of Industrial Production. We employ a linear probability model to link firm characteristics to the likelihood of remaining under state control. We undertake this exercise for two time intervals: 1998–2002, a period following massive urban state-owned enterprise (SOE) restructuring and significant labor unrest; and 2002–2006, the early years of the Hu administration.[1] We then summarize the findings of recent analyses of restructuring's success in reducing factor misallocations and, hence, its contribution to productivity growth. Finally, we use our analysis of the grasp-or-release decision to highlight some of the challenges of continued SOE reforms.

OWNERSHIP RESTRUCTURING, ENTERPRISE CLASSIFICATION, AND THE EXTENT OF STATE CONTROL IN THE INDUSTRIAL SECTOR

Identification and measurement of the Chinese "state sector" are complicated by the variety of ways in which state-controlled firms are organized. According to Gan (2009), SOE restructuring stems from policies initiated in the 1980s and early 1990 permitting changes to enterprise governance structures rather than outright privatization. The formal adoption of the Company Law in 1994 provided a legal framework into which different ownership forms could fit. The law permitted the formal conversion of state-owned enterprises to joint stock companies, allowing for the option of selling off some or all shares of the new organization (Naughton 2007, p. 301). Shareholding conversion, called "corporatization" when the state retains a controlling interest, became a broad-based initiative after 1997 when the Chinese Communist Party's Fifteenth Congress elevated the shareholding system as a vehicle for enterprise restructuring. The changing ownership composition was also shaped by the adoption at the Fifteenth Party Congress of the policy known as "grasping the large, letting go of the small" (Gan, Guo, and Xu 2015). This policy sought to protect and promote the largest, typically centrally controlled, state enterprises while spurring the privatization or exit of smaller, often loss-making, enterprises controlled by lower levels of government. The policy quickly led to dramatic changes in China's industrial sector. Jefferson et al. (2005) find that from 1997 to 2001 the number of large and medium-sized SOEs declined by over 40 percent, and the number of large and medium-sized collective enterprises declined by 35 percent, while the number of shareholding firms soared.

These policies resulted in a distinct blurring of boundaries between state-controlled and privately held enterprises. Since 2001, the evolution of the Chinese industrial sector has continued, but tracking the extent to which state control has receded is difficult. China's National Bureau of Statistics assigns each firm an ownership classification, known as its "registration status." State-owned enterprises include those that are majority owned by the central government or a local government, those registered to the state but jointly operated with a nonstate entity, and those wholly state owned. Private firms, by registration status, include those registered to natural persons, whether solely, in partnership, as limited liability enterprises, or shareholding firms. Distinctions between ownership types become truly opaque in another type of domestic registration status, legal persons. Firms registered as legal persons include limited liability and shareholding limited liability firms. Their relationship to the state is not indicated by their registration status. An additional complication is that the state may control firms in which it has only a minority holding, firms that are correctly registered as private or foreign owned. These complexities imply that measures of the state-controlled industrial share drawn from aggregate statistics based on registration type are misleading.

Enterprises registered as legal persons are mostly shareholding firms, an organizational form integral to reform of China's state-owned enterprises (Jefferson et al. 2005). Shareholding firms may operate under state control, may be privately controlled, or may simply be "hybrid ownership." Fortunately, progress in identifying firms not classified as SOEs by registration status yet controlled by the state can be made by accessing additional information contained in China's Annual Survey of Industrial Production (ASIP). This census of all state-owned enterprises and other industrial firms with revenues above 5 million RMB is available to us for the period 1998–2006 only. The ASIP includes information on the origin of the various sources of registered capital in the firm—the state, collectives, legal persons, private persons, and foreigners.[2] This information on equity shares can be used to classify firms based on majority ownership. If 50 percent or more of equity originates from state, collective, private, or foreign sources, the enterprise can be reclassified accordingly. However, for many firms, legal person is a significant source of capital, making it impossible to classify these firms based on paid-in capital shares alone. Indeed, of the 54,320 firms officially registered as legal person, 21,910 enterprises cannot be reclassified using equity information because the majority of their capital originates from a legal person. In other words, equity shares do not allow us to completely peer around the veil of legal-person status.

Other researchers have faced this problem. Dollar and Wei (2007) add legal-person capital to private capital before calculating majority ownership. While subsequent researchers have followed the same procedure, this method ignores Huang's (2008) observation that categorizing legal-person firms as private can be misleading because "(e)ven a casual glance at the data reveals that many of these legal-person shareholding firms are among the best-known and quintessential SOEs in China" (p. 16). Huang concludes that "(t)he majority of the shareholding firms, especially the large ones, are still state-controlled" (p. 46). His observation suggests that an alternative grouping of firms, in which legal-person capital is treated as state-owned capital before calculating majority ownership, is also reasonable.[3] Kamal and Lovely (2013) take a middle approach in their study of labor misallocation: they separate legal-person enterprises from both SOEs and firms registered as privately owned.

Fortunately, the ASIP contains additional information that defines the firm's controlling shareholder as either the state, a collective, a foreigner, or a private person. Together with data on equity shares, the ASIP allows us to define state-owned and state-controlled (SOSC) firms. We define a firm as SOSC when it is registered as an SOE, when the share of registered capital held directly by the state exceeds or equals 50 percent, or when the state is reported as the controlling shareholder. The method captures those firms registered as SOEs and those in which the state holds a controlling interest, whether directly or through a holding company. Hsieh and Song (2015) use a similar method to identify state-controlled firms, and they report that this method resulted in correct categorization when they manually checked the results using information directly from firm websites.[4]

To identify enterprises that remain under state control from those that transition to another type of ownership, we need to trace firms over time. However, linking firms across years can be problematic because firm IDs may be changed or missing when there are revisions in legal registration status. We follow Brandt, Van Biesebroeck, and Zhang's (2012) method of constructing complete firm histories. We supplement matching via the firm's Legal Person Entity Code with matching based on five additional identifiers: firm name, industry code, geographic code, founding year, and name of main product. After completing this multistep procedure, we can match over time more than 95 percent of the firms in the data set.

The state sector appears to recede far less when corporatized yet state-controlled firms are included in the definition of state enterprises rather than considered private firms. Figure 5.1 shows trends in the share of total enterprises by type of ownership. When ownership is defined using NBS registration status, the number of state-owned enterprises falls by more than 90 percent between 1998 and 2006, accounting for only about 3 percent of all above-scale firms by 2006.[5] However, using information on equity shares to define ownership allows us to observe another 1 percent of firms as being state majority owned in 2006. We also find an additional 1 percent of firms for which ownership cannot be determined directly from paid-in capital shares but which are identified

Figure 5.1 Shares of Total Enterprises, by Type of State Control

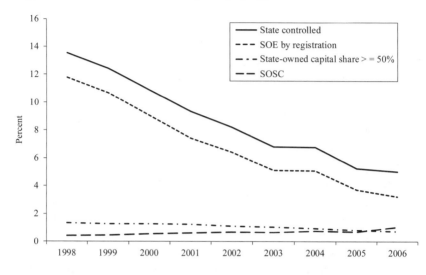

SOURCE: Authors' calculations.

as state controlled by the NBS. In total, we find that about 5 percent of total enterprises are state owned and controlled in 2006.

If these adjustments seem too small to bother with, Table 5.1 shows that the state controls a much larger share of industrial output than the number of firms might suggest. As seen in Figure 5.2, firms registered as SOEs account for 15 percent of gross industrial output, even though they make up only 3 percent of all enterprises. Similarly, corporatized firms controlled by the state punch above their numbers due to their larger than average size. Firms in which the state owns 50 percent or more of registered capital provide 5.4 percent of gross output, while firms controlled by the state without having registered majority state ownership account for fully 11 percent of gross output. Altogether, as shown in Figure 5.2, SOSC enterprises provided 31.4 percent of gross industrial output by 2006, more than double the share produced by registered SOEs, and that the decline in state share appears to level out by 2005.

Figure 5.3 shows trends in output shares for SOSC firms, distinguished by their official registration type. While about 60 percent of state-controlled firms are registered as SOEs, the share of SOSC firms

Table 5.1 Enterprise Size and Performance: Linear Probability Model of Firm Remaining State Controlled or State Owned, 1998–2002 and 2002–2006

	1998–2002		2002–2006	
	(1)	(2)	(3)	(4)
ln Output value	0.0506***	0.0472***	0.0606***	0.0481***
(normed)	(0.00299)	(0.00541)	(0.00241)	(0.00740)
ln Viability	0.0491***	0.0329***	0.0352***	0.0275***
	(0.00475)	(0.00456)	(0.00661)	(0.00611)
ln Return on	−0.0326***	−0.0258***	−0.0340***	−0.0157***
assets	(0.00428)	(0.00465)	(0.00544)	(0.00480)
Observations	55,502	55,502	35,719	35,719
Industry fixed effects	No	Yes	No	Yes

NOTE: *p < 0.1; **p < 0.05; ***p < 0.01. Dependent variable takes value of 1 if firm remains state owned or state controlled over full-time period. Robust standard errors in parentheses are clustered at the two-digit census industry code.
SOURCE: Authors' calculations.

registered as limited liability corporations grew dramatically after 2001. Recognizing that firms officially registered as legal-person enterprises are larger than average, properly classifying these organizational forms is integral to tracking the extent of state control in China's industrial sector. Proper classification leads to quite different conclusions about the extent of "privatization" from that drawn using registration type alone. We conclude that the Chinese state continues to control firms supplying more than 30 percent of industrial output and that earlier downward trends in the state share appear to level off by 2005.

GRASPING AND RELEASING

Large-scale restructuring of China's state-owned firms began in the late 1990s. As we have shown, this process resulted in a smaller share of firms owned by the state. With about a third of gross industrial output still under state control, however, we now examine the characteristics of those enterprises chosen by the state to be released and which it

Figure 5.2   Shares of Gross Industrial Output Value, by Type of State Control

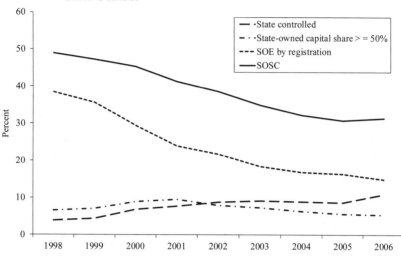

SOURCE: Authors' calculations.

Figure 5.3   Shares by Registration Type among State-Owned, State-Controlled Enterprises

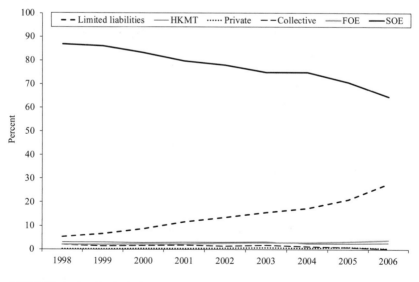

SOURCE: Authors' calculations.

chose to grasp. Such an analysis provides insight into both the process of sculpting the modern state sector in China, and also the problems that continued to face the state industrial sector after 2006.

The slogan "grasp the large, let go of the small" suggests that enterprise performance was a major determinant of decisions about industrial restructuring. Naughton (2007) reports that "In 'grasping the large,' policymakers sought to focus their attention on the largest, typically centrally controlled firms" (p. 31). In addition to size, the financial status of the firm likely contributed to the retention decision. An impetus for selling assets, especially at the local level, was the negative budgetary impact associated with loss-making and insolvent enterprises. Firms with debts in excess of the value of their assets were essentially bankrupt. Because of "soft budget constraints" in the period before restructuring, enterprises could lose money for a prolonged period yet continue to receive financing and investment. These injections of funds sapped the resources of local governments and contributed to concerns about government indebtedness. As reported by Gan, Guo, and Xu (2015, p. 7), by the late 1990s, "the deteriorating performance of SOEs put increasing pressure on the fiscal conditions of local governments because they are the residual claimants of the SOE earnings and some were on the verge of insolvency following the losses of their SOEs."

While selling off the shares of insolvent firms may have solved the government's problem, finding buyers for such firms would be difficult without some indication that the firm could be profitable. Consequently, profitability may also have been a factor in determining which enterprises the state retained, with better-performing firms being sold while others were held under various organizational forms. We can summarize these enterprise performance criteria for retaining a firm under state control in the following hypothesis:

H1: The Chinese state was more likely to retain control of an enterprise that, ceteris paribus, was larger, financially viable, and less profitable. These factors matter in both time periods, 1998–2002 and 2002–2006.

To test this hypothesis, we measure the size, viability, and profitability of each firm in the initial year of each time period. Table 5.2 provides descriptive statistics for all variables used in our regression analysis. We measure enterprise size as the gross value of industrial output of the firm relative to the average output value of private firms in the same three-digit industry. Viability is measured as the ratio for the firm of total current assets to total current liabilities. Lastly, we use sales revenue divided by total assets of the enterprise as a measure of firm profitability.

Some observers express the view that privatization was shaped by a desire to continue to guide economic development through the allocation of resources to sectors with strategic importance. Naughton (2007) states that the central government concentrated its focus on energy, natural resources, and other industries with large economies of scale. These upstream industries provide inputs into many different industrial activities and thus have strategic importance in driving economic development. The state may then have sought to retain control of firms in the upstream industries.

While local governments were given de jure control rights for local SOEs in 1997, the pressures they faced to restructure were associated with their own resources and assets. Lower levels of government held assets that may have been deemed less strategically important and more tempting to use as a source of revenue. Gan, Guo, and Xu (2015) find that direct sales of firm assets to insiders was the method of privatization used most often by local governments to release local SOEs from state control. This method of privatization is the most controversial because it lacks transparency and may result in the underpricing of state assets. Thus, local governments may have found SOEs under their jurisdiction less strategically important to retain and more tempting to sell off. We can summarize these strategic importance perspectives on state control in the following hypothesis:

H2: The Chinese state was more likely to retain control of an enterprise that, ceteris paribus, was further upstream in the industrial sector and was affiliated with a higher level of government.

To measure strategic importance, we control for the degree of "upstreamness" of the three-digit industry to which the enterprise belongs. We measure this industry characteristic using the upstream index for two-digit sectors created by Tang, Wang, and Wang (2016) for China using the method of Antras et al. (2012). The index essentially measures the number of industries between a producer and the final consumer, with a higher number indicating that the firm has a

Table 5.2 Description of Variables Used in Regression Analysis

	Description	Mean 1998–2002	Mean 2002–2006
State owned or state controlled	=1 if start as SOSC and remain SOSC to end of period (see text for definition of SOSC)	0.45 (0.50)	0.39 (0.49)
ln Output value (normed)	Log of output value divided by averaged private firm's output value in same 3-digit industry	−1.38 (2.10)	−1.31 (2.09)
ln Viability	Log of total current assets divided by total current liabilities	−0.16 (0.82)	−0.13 (0.94)
ln Return on assets	Log of industrial sales revenue divided by total assets	−1.04 (1.24)	−0.95 (1.31)
Social burden	Log of the ratio of firm's industrial sales per worker to the averaged industrial sales per worker in the same 3-digit industry	−1.44 (1.36)	−1.25 (1.37)
Strategic burden	Log of ratio of industry's total export values to industry's total domestic sales	−2.84 (1.63)	−2.91 (1.61)
Upstream index	From Tang, Wang, and Wang (2014)	3.30 (0.55)	3.33 (0.56)
Central affiliated	Enterprise affiliated with central government	0.07 (0.25)	0.09 (0.28)
Province affiliated	Enterprise affiliated with a provincial government	0.13 (0.33)	0.17 (0.38)
City affiliated	Enterprise affiliated with a city government	0.25 (0.43)	0.25 (0.43)
Private competition	Share of output in 3-digit industry from private enterprises	0.04 (0.03)	0.13 (0.10)
Foreign-invested enterprise competition	Share of output in 3-digit industry from foreign-invested enterprises	0.11 (0.09)	0.12 (0.11)
Central state-owned enterprise competition	Share of output in 3-digit industry from state-owned enterprises	0.09 (0.16)	0.08 (0.16)

NOTE: Standard deviations are in parentheses.
SOURCE: Data drawn from China's NBS Annual Survey of Industrial Production.

more upstream location in the production chain. We also include a set of dummy variables indicating the level of government with which the enterprise is affiliated. The ASIP contains this information, distinguishing between central, provincial, city, or town government affiliation.

The last set of explanations for privatization decisions refers to what we can term "legacy burdens." These burdens reflect the use of state enterprises to achieve goals other than production and take three forms: social burdens, strategic burdens, and competitive burdens. Because these burdens reduce the efficiency and profitability of state enterprises, they distinguish firms that may be difficult to sell off without prior restructuring and that fill an important and continuing social obligation.

Prior to the mid-1990s, state enterprises often served to ensure full employment in urban areas, a responsibility for social stability termed the "social burden" by Lin (2012). Cai, Park, and Zhao (2008) explain that SOE managers were prohibited from firing urban workers and that municipal governments continued to place workers into state-sector jobs well into the 1990s even when they were not required. We hypothesize that excess staffing would contribute to the desirability of privatizing a firm to increase productivity, but the problem of uninsured and unemployed workers would remain. Indeed, Lin argues that much of this responsibility remains today with SOEs, who still shoulder a social burden.

Another burden identified by Lin (2012) is what he terms the "strategic burden." This handicap resulted from the presence of state enterprises in sectors deemed strategically important for economic development but not in line with China's comparative advantage. These enterprises would not be viable without significant state support, including competitive restrictions. To the extent that the state continues to seek industrial upgrading, they may have retained control of enterprises in these "comparative-advantage-defying" industries.

A final burden for state enterprises flows from a competitive squeeze experienced by local SOEs operating in sectors dominated by foreign-invested firms and large, centrally controlled SOEs. These enterprises may not be able to withstand the pressure of more advanced competitors and, thus, may be allowed to go bankrupt or be sold.

We can summarize these legacy-burden considerations in the following hypothesis.

H3: The Chinese state was more likely to retain control of an enterprise if, ceteris paribus, it bore a larger social burden; it bore a strategic burden related to comparative disadvantage; it was subject to a competitive squeeze from foreign firms and large SOEs.

To measure the social burden borne by a firm, we create an index of overstaffing based on average labor productivity in the industry. Specifically, we calculate sales revenue per employee in each given firm and divide by the average sales per employee in the firm's three-digit industry. Higher values of the index indicate that the firm has a higher labor productivity relative to the average firm in the industry. The strategic burden reflects an industry's comparative advantage, so we create an industry-level measure based on the ratio of export sales to total domestic sales. Higher values of this measure indicate that the industry has strong international sales. Lastly, we control for the competitive squeeze by including the market share in each three-digit industry of private firms, foreign-invested enterprises, and centrally affiliated SOEs.

REGRESSION RESULTS

To test our hypotheses, we estimate a linear probability model of the likelihood that a state enterprise remains active and state controlled by the end of the period.[6] Our dependent variable takes the value of unity if an initially state-controlled firm remains state controlled, using the method of classifying enterprises as SOSC described above, until the last year in the interval. Since China experienced a change of regime (President Hu took office in December 2002) and reemphasized deepening SOE reform in the 16th CPC Plenary Session, we divide our sample into two periods. The sample contains 67,509 initially state-controlled firms for the period 1998–2002 and 40,857 initially state-controlled firms for the period 2002–2006.

Table 5.1 provides the results of the linear probability estimation, including only those variables related to firm performance. We use these results to test the hypothesis that the government was more likely to retain control of an enterprise that, ceteris paribus, was larger, financially viable, and less profitable. For each period we provide estimates with and without the inclusion of an industry fixed effect.

As seen in Table 5.1, all three firm performance indicators are significant determinants of state retention. The estimated coefficient on enterprise size, normed by average industry output value, is positive and highly significant in both time periods. The coefficient, when estimated with industry fixed effects, is of very similar magnitude in both periods. A 1 percent increase in a firm's output value relative to the industry average, all else equal, raises the probability that it is retained by the state by about 5 percentage points.

A firm's financial viability, measured as the ratio of its assets to its liabilities, is also a significant determinant of state retention. When we include industry fixed effects, the estimated coefficient implies that a 1 percent increase in this ratio raises the probability that the state maintains control by about 3 percentage points. This finding is consistent with the view that the state sold off enterprises that were bankrupt.

Our last indicator of firm performance is ROA, the ratio of firm revenues to assets. The estimated coefficient is negative and highly significant, even when we include industry fixed effects. A 1 percent increase in this revenue ratio reduces the likelihood of state retention by 2.6 percentage points over the period 1998–2002 and by 1.6 points over the period 2002–2006. This finding is consistent with state retention of underperforming assets. In the data set, 45 percent of initially SOSC firms remain state controlled by 2002 and 39 percent by 2006, so the magnitudes of the marginal effects on retention decisions of all three firm performance factors appear to be both economically and statistically significant.

We extend our analysis with the results shown in Table 5.3, which provides coefficient estimates obtained by adding the strategic importance characteristics to our linear probability model. We hypothesize that the Chinese state was more likely to retain control of an enterprise that, ceteris paribus, was further upstream in the industrial sector and was affiliated with a higher level of government. Since our upstream index is an industry characteristic, we do not include industry fixed effects in these models.

Surprisingly, we find that the upstreamness of the firm's industry is not significantly correlated with the probability of state retention in either period. Moreover, the level of governmental affiliation has no significant relation to retained control over the period 1998–2002, during which the Chinese Communist Party's Central Committee had the

Table 5.3 Strategic Centrality: Linear Probability Model of Firm Remaining State Controlled or State Owned, 1998–2002 and 2002–2006

	1998–2002		2002–2006	
	(1)	(2)	(3)	(4)
ln Output value	0.0533***	0.0458***	0.0588***	0.0474***
(normed)	(0.00270)	(0.00239)	(0.00399)	(0.00390)
ln Viability	0.0467***	0.0345***	0.0489***	0.0321***
	(0.00471)	(0.00291)	(0.00472)	(0.00393)
ln Return on assets	−0.0350***	−0.0272***	−0.0269***	−0.0145***
	(0.00439)	(0.00374)	(0.00410)	(0.00391)
Upstream index	0.0150	−0.00899	0.0164	−0.00222
	(0.0197)	(0.0101)	(0.0228)	(0.0115)
Central affiliated		0.144		0.216**
		(0.150)		(0.0939)
Province affiliated		0.117		0.167***
		(0.0913)		(0.0510)
City affiliated		−0.00493		0.0745
		(0.0488)		(0.0458)
Observations	43,819	43,819	24,686	24,686
Industry fixed effects	No	No	No	No

NOTE: *p < 0.1; **p < 0.05; ***p < 0. 01. Dependent variable takes value of 1 if firm remains state owned or state controlled over full time period. Robust standard errors in parentheses are clustered at the two-digit census industry code.
SOURCE: Authors' calculations.

political support necessary to issue an official policy statement on the urgency of reform of state-owned enterprises (Central Committee of the Communist Party of China 1999). Our results suggest that the party was then able to align the direction of reform at all levels of government.

During the first years of the Hu administration, however, the level of state affiliation appears to have become a powerful determinant of whether a firm remained under state control. Being affiliated with the central government raised the likelihood of remaining state controlled by an estimated 21.6 percentage points, while affiliation with a province or provincial-level city raised the likelihood of retention by 16.7 percent, both measured relative to the likelihood of retention of firms affiliated with city or town governments. These estimated magnitudes are quite large and suggest that corporatization, rather than privatization, became the mode of choice for higher-level governments seeking to improve the performance of their state assets. Enterprises associated with local governments were more likely to be privatized or closed, all else equal, than those affiliated with higher levels.

Table 5.4 provides additional results that include measures of the legacy burdens faced by each state-controlled firm. We hypothesize that an enterprise was more likely to be retained if it bore a larger social burden, bore a strategic burden related to comparative disadvantage, and was subject to a competitive squeeze from foreign firms and large SOEs. Among all these factors, our results suggest that only the social burden is a significant determinant of state privatization decisions. Estimate coefficients for the strategic burden variable, defined as the export success of the firm's industry, and all measures of the competitive squeeze faced by local SOEs are statistically insignificant in both periods. In contrast, the coefficient for social burden is significant in both periods. Defined as the firm's sales per worker relative to the average sales per worker in the industry, social burden is a measure of relative labor productivity. Our results indicate that a 1 percent increase in this ratio reduces the likelihood of state retention by 2.7 percentage points in the first period, 1998–2002, and by 0.8 points in the second period, 2002–2006. Essentially, firms with better labor productivity were more likely to be privatized or exit than to remain state controlled. This finding supports the view that restructuring did not discharge all SOE social burdens and that the state sector continues to some extent to bear the legacy of social stability goals, as argued by Lin (2012).

STATE RESTRUCTURING AND ECONOMIC PERFORMANCE

Our regression analysis indicates that larger, more financially stable firms, especially those affiliated with higher levels of government, were more likely to remain under state control. We also find that the state was less likely to shed enterprises with low labor productivity. These patterns are consistent with the creation of a state sector comprising firms with dominant industry positions but possibly weak performance. Explicit comparison of state firms to nonstate firms, a task that has recently been undertaken by several groups of researchers, is important

Table 5.4 Legacy Burdens and Competitive Squeeze: Linear Probability Model of Firm Remaining State Controlled or State Owned, 1998–2002 and 2002–2006

	1998–2002		2002–2006	
	(1)	(2)	(3)	(4)
ln Output value	0.0541***	0.0545***	0.0507***	0.0508***
(normed)	(0.00290)	(0.00296)	(0.00429)	(0.00433)
ln Viability	0.0387***	0.0379***	0.0332***	0.0324***
	(0.00401)	(0.00391)	(0.00420)	(0.00385)
ln Return on assets	−0.0155***	−0.0158***	−0.0111***	−0.0111***
	(0.00316)	(0.00339)	(0.00378)	(0.00384)
Upstream index	−0.00814	−0.00954	−0.00334	0.000485
	(0.0106)	(0.0128)	(0.0126)	(0.0142)
Central affiliated	0.161	0.132	0.205*	0.199***
	(0.171)	(0.159)	(0.101)	(0.0559)
Province affiliated	0.147	0.134	0.152***	0.145***
	(0.105)	(0.102)	(0.0515)	(0.0514)
City affiliated	0.00551	−0.00277	0.0669	0.0637
	(0.0624)	(0.0611)	(0.0432)	(0.0386)
Social burden	−0.0273***	−0.0271***	−0.00887**	−0.00853**
	(0.00471)	(0.00471)	(0.00390)	(0.00363)
Strategic burden	−0.0102	−0.0100	0.00196	−0.00130
	(0.00884)	(0.00902)	(0.00570)	(0.00738)
Private competition		0.0775		0.0269
		(0.183)		(0.0865)
Foreign-invested		0.0132		0.0928
competition		(0.0839)		(0.0935)
State-owned enter-		0.121*		0.0147
prise competition		(0.0588)		(0.132)
Observations	40,317	40,317	24,686	24,686
Industry fixed effects	No	No	No	No

NOTE: *$p < 0.1$; **$p < 0.05$; ***$p < 0.01$. Dependent variable takes value of 1 if firm remains state owned or state controlled over full time period. Robust standard errors in parentheses are clustered at the two-digit census industry code.
SOURCE: Authors' calculations.

because if factor productivity is systematically related to state status, and if inputs are allocated to state-controlled enterprises in a discriminatory manner, the economy will not perform at its full potential.

Performance gaps between SOEs and other types of firms were present early in the reform process: Brandt, Tombe, and Zhu (2013) find significant productivity differences between the state and the nonstate in nonagricultural sectors from 1985 to 2007. By their estimates, over the entire period, misallocation of factors between the state and nonstate sectors and across provinces lowered aggregate nonagricultural total factor productivity (TFP) by an average of 20 percent. Interestingly, given the massive layoffs of state workers beginning in the mid-1990s, these losses—after initially declining—increased appreciably as retrenchment expanded. Brandt, Tombe, and Zhu attribute these trends almost exclusively to increasing misallocation of capital between state and nonstate sectors caused by contemporaneous government policies that encouraged investments in state enterprises at the expense of investments in the more productive nonstate sector.

Hsieh and Klenow (2009) also emphasize the systematic distortions caused by preferential access to capital in their assessment of the economic cost of an inefficient state sector. Relying on firm-level data to calculate total factor productivity, measured by revenue productivity, for Chinese firms over the period 1998–2005, they find that state-owned firms exhibit 41 percent lower TFP than nonstate firms, an outcome consistent with the provision of subsidies to these firms to remain active. These findings agree with Dollar and Wei (2007), who also find lower productivity at state-owned firms in China during this time.

Misallocation of labor has also been found by researchers using Chinese microdata. Fleisher et al. (2011) find that the marginal product of both highly and less-educated workers is lower in SOEs than in domestic private or foreign-invested firms. Kamal and Lovely (2013) also focus on the allocation of labor across enterprises with a special emphasis on how SOEs compare to enterprises owned by legal persons, a category that includes "corporatized" state-owned firms. They calculate the marginal revenue product of labor for all firms in the ASIP during two periods, 2001–2004 and 2004–2007. They find that labor productivity varies systematically within industries by ownership type and that all organizational forms, on average, exhibit higher labor productivities than do SOEs. Indeed, labor in enterprises registered as legal persons had a higher average product than labor employed in private firms. Kamal and Lovely also find that labor productivity differentials fell over time, with the gap between SOEs and other firm types falling by about half between the two periods they analyze.

Several recent studies account for the sources of China's economic growth, attempting to discern the particular contribution of SOE restructuring. Brandt, Van Biesebroeck, and Zhang (2012) estimate TFP at the firm level using the ASIP for the period 1998–2007. They find that the main source of growing aggregate TFP is productivity improvement in continuing firms and the entry of new firms with higher productivity. They also find that large Chinese firms increased productivity at a faster than average rate, and the restructuring of large state-owned firms was one driver for this pattern. The authors identify an important dynamic as the state sector receded: "The relative success in attracting new input factors determined relative growth rates. New state firms that appeared between 1998 and 2007 were able to produce almost five times as much value-added as disappearing state firms, even though their real capital stock only grew marginally and employment was a quarter lower" (p. 35). Despite this positive dynamic pattern, Brandt, Van Biesebroeck, and Zhang suggest that biases in favor of state-connected firms likely depressed productivity growth after 2007.

Hsieh and Song (2015) measure the quantitative importance of the restructuring policies pursued from 1998 to 2007 on aggregate productivity growth. They find that reforms were potentially responsible for 20 percent of aggregate output by 2007. Explicitly comparing surviving state-owned firms to those that were privatized, Hsieh and Song find that for both types the labor productivity gap with surviving private firms narrowed, a finding consistent with Kamal and Lovely (2013), while the capital productivity gap narrowed by much less. Indeed, their estimates indicate that as late as 2007, capital productivity of state-owned firms was less than 50 percent of private firms.

In light of our estimates, the lower productivity of state-controlled firms appears a natural consequence of how enterprises were grasped and released. Our linear probability model estimates suggest that the state was more likely to retain control of firms that produced low revenues relative to assets and that exhibited relatively low labor productivity. The picture that emerges is one in which the state sector was shaped by retention of firms that required continued preferential access to capital and that suffered from the failure to develop adequate alternative policies for redundant workers. It is not surprising, therefore, that average state sector productivity continued to lag behind the private sector, despite innovation in the form of state control.

CHALLENGES FOR THE FUTURE

After several decades of retrenchment, the Chinese state remains a dominant player in several strategic industries. State-controlled enterprises provide most of the output in the heavy industries, including oil production and distribution, minerals and mining, steel, shipbuilding, and transportation equipment. The state also continues to control important pieces of the service sector: construction, utilities, financial services, media, and air travel and logistics.

The outlook for the foreseeable future is one in which the Chinese state continues to play a major role in the economy. Hsieh and Song (2015) find that after 2005, privatization rates declined on average even though they increased for small firms. Based on an analysis of industry-level data, they also suggest that there was little convergence in capital productivity from 2007 to 2012. This finding suggests a continuing cost in terms of lost national income, especially since, according to China's NBS, "state-owned and controlled enterprises" accounted for 41 percent of fixed asset investment from 2004 to 2012.

A recent study from Goldman Sachs Investment Strategy Group (2016) also supports the view that the return on state sector assets continues to lag. They report that "about 150,000 SOEs control over $15 trillion of assets in China, which in aggregate and excluding financial institutions returned 2.4 percent as of 2014" (p. 26). This return on assets can be compared to a 3.1 percent return estimated for comparable Chinese listed companies and 6.4 percent for U.S. companies. These numbers indicate continuing low profitability for Chinese SOEs.

Aside from lost productivity, continued differential investment into state enterprises may make the goal of macroeconomic rebalancing more difficult to achieve. To raise consumption, Chinese households must receive a larger share of aggregate income. However, while some parts of the state sector are very profitable, almost none of this profit is returned to the public for services or to reduce taxes. Rather, it is reinvested by the state sector. The likely response of households to this continuing pattern is to continue to hold high savings balances. Because continued investment in the state sector produces low returns or is non-productive, households may guard against the effect of future financial repression by saving for future higher taxes or service cuts. Investment in the state sector, in this sense, conflicts with the goal of pivoting the economy toward consumption-led growth.

In 2015, the CPC Central Committee and State Council issued guidelines for SOE reform emphasizing the desire for "mixed owner-ship," with private investors becoming shareholders in state-controlled firms (*Xinhua* 2015). Our analysis of the history of grasping and releas-ing suggests that the state will continue to control the largest firms, especially those affiliated with higher levels of government, in a variety of forms. Our review of recent assessments of the role of SOE reform in China's growth suggests that significant productivity gains have stemmed from privatization and corporatization. Despite these gains, however, SOEs as a whole continue to provide subpar returns on assets while receiving a disproportionate share of total investment. How much more their performance can be enhanced by further promotion of mixed ownership without full privatization remains an open question.

Notes

1. To flag wavering commitment to continued adjustment, a policy directive was issued in 1999 emphasizing the urgency of continued SOE reforms. See Central Committee of the Communist Party of China (1999).
2. Foreign-owned includes capital from Hong Kong, Macao, Taiwan, and all other foreign sources.
3. Other methods for classifying firms have also been used. For example, Brandt, Van Biesebroeck, and Zhang (2012) use equity shares to classify firms as state, private, or hybrid.
4. Hsieh and Song (2015) do not select firms based on registration type, whereas we include registered SOEs as SOSC firms. This difference in method makes only a minor difference in the resulting state share estimates, as registered capital held by the state in most registered SOEs exceeds 50 percent.
5. Collective enterprises also declined sharply in number, falling 85 percent over the period. In contrast, firms registered as private enterprises rose sharply—the num-ber of private firms grew 670 percent and constituted over half of all above-scale firms by 2006. The number of firms registered as legal persons, most of which are

shareholding enterprises, rose 160 percent by 2006. See Kamal and Lovely (2013) for more details.

6. A drawback of the linear probability model is that the estimated coefficients can imply probabilities outside the unit interval [0,1]. The model also implies constant marginal effects. We use the linear probability model here because the coefficient values permit straightforward interpretation. When we use a logit model, our qualitative results remain unchanged.

References

Antras, Pol, Daviin Chor, Thibault Fally, and Russell Hillberry. 2012. "Measuring the Upstreamness of Production and Trade Flows." *American Economic Review Papers and Proceedings* 102(3): 412–416.

Brandt, Loren, Johannes Van Biesebroeck, and Yifan Zhang. 2012. "Creative Accounting or Creative Destruction? Firm-level Productivity Growth in Chinese Manufacturing." *Journal of Development Economics* 97(2): 339–351.

Brandt, Loren, Trevor Tombe, and Xiadong Zhu. 2013. "Factor Market Distortions across Time, Space, and Sectors in China." *Review of Economic Dynamics* 16(1): 39–58.

Cai, Fang, Albert Park, and Yaohui Zhao. 2008. "The Chinese Labor Market in the Reform Era." In *China's Great Economic Transformation*, Loren Brandt and Thomas G. Rawski, eds. New York: Cambridge University Press, pp. 167–214.

Central Committee of the Communist Party of China. 1999. "The Decision of the Central Committee of the Communist Party of China on Major Issues Concerning the Reform and Development of State-Owned Enterprises." Adopted at the Fourth Plenum of the Fifteenth Communist Party of China Central Committee on September 22. http://en.pkulaw.cn/display.aspx?cgid=23496&lib=law (accessed May 2, 2017).

Dollar, David, and Shang-Jin Wei. 2007. "Das (Wasted) Kapital: Firm Ownership and Investment Efficiency in China." NBER Working Paper No. 13103. Cambridge, MA: National Bureau of Economic Research.

Fleisher, Belton M., Yifan Hu, Haizheng Li, and Seonghoon Kim. 2011. "Economic Transition, Higher Education, and Worker Productivity in China." *Journal of Development Economics* 94(1): 86–94.

Gan, Jie. 2009. "Privatization in China: Experiences and Lesson." In *China's Emerging Financial Markets: Challenges and Opportunities*, James R. Barth, John A. Tatom, and Glenn Yago, eds. New York: Springer, pp. 581–592.

Gan, Jie, Yan Guo, and Cheng-Gang Xu. 2015. "China's Decentralized Privatization and Change of Control Rights." CEPR Discussion Paper No. DP10331. London: Centre for Economic Policy Research.

Goldman Sachs Investment Strategy Group. 2016. *Walled In: China's Great Dilemma*. New York: Goldman Sachs, Investment Management Division. http://www.goldmansachs.com/what-we-do/investment-management/private-wealth-management/intellectual-capital/isg-china-insight-2016.pdf (accessed May 3, 2017).

Hsieh, Chang-Tai, and Peter J. Klenow. 2009. "Misallocation and Manufacturing TFP in China and India." *Quarterly Journal of Economics* 124(4): 1403–1448.

Hsieh, Chang-Tai, and Zheng (Michael) Song. 2015. "Grasp the Large, Let Go of the Small: The Transformation of the State Sector in China." *Brookings Papers on Economic Activity* (Spring): 295–346.

Huang, Yasheng. 2008. *Capitalism with Chinese Characteristics: Entrepreneurship and the State*. New York: Cambridge University Press.

Jefferson, Gary H., Su Jian, Jiang Yuan, and Yu Xinhua. 2005. "China's Shareholding Reform: Effects on Enterprise Performance." In *Reality Check: The Distributional Impact of Privatization in Developing Countries*, John Nellis and Nancy Birdsall, eds. Washington, DC: Center for Global Development, pp. 353–388.

Kamal, Fariha, and Mary E. Lovely. 2013. "Labor Allocation in China: Implicit Taxation of the Heterogeneous Non-State Sector." *CESifo Economic Studies* 59(4): 731–758.

Kowalski, Przemyslaw, Max Büge, Monica Sztajerowska, and Matias Egeland. 2013. "State-Owned Enterprises: Trade Effects and Policy Implications." OECD Trade Policy Paper No. 147. Paris: Organisation for Economic Co-operation and Development.

Lardy, Nicholas R. 2014. *Markets over Mao: The Rise of Private Business in China*. Washington, DC: Peterson Institute for International Economics.

Lin, Justin Yifu. 2012. *Demystifying the Chinese Economy*. Cambridge: Cambridge University Press.

Naughton, Barry J. 2007. *The Chinese Economy: Transitions and Growth*. Cambridge, MA: MIT Press.

Nee, Victor, and Sonja Opper. 2012. *Capitalism from Below: Markets and Institutional Change in China*. Cambridge, MA: Harvard University Press.

Tang, Heiwai, Fei Wang, and Zhi Wang. 2016. "The Domestic Segment of Global Value Chains in China." Unpublished paper. Washington, DC: School of Advanced International Studies, Johns Hopkins University.

Xinhua. 2015. "China Issues Guidelines to Deepen SOE Reforms." September 13. www.xinhuanet.com+c_134620039.htm (accessed June 17, 2017).

6

Why Exit Rights Are the Key to the Reduction of Urban-Rural Income Disparity in China

Guanzhong James Wen
Trinity College

Since the adoption of the "open up and reform" policy in 1978, China has reached many economic milestones. Until recently, it had maintained an average growth rate that was not only higher but also longer than almost any other nation in modern history (Naughton and Tsai 2015).

China is now the second-largest economy and is poised to become the largest in a not too distant future. It currently holds the largest foreign reserves, producing almost half of the world's total steel and coal, and is the biggest producer of many important industrial products. However, China also has been facing some challenges. This chapter discusses the following issues:

- The change in China's social structure has been lingering much more slowly behind that in its economic structure, resulting in relatively impoverished farmers and migrant workers, languorous rural communities, and an inefficient farming sector compared with its urban areas.

- Two institutional barriers will result in a middle-income trap through exclusive urbanization: the hukou system and the compulsory collective land ownership.

- The reasons it is impossible for China to develop a real land market under its Constitutional stipulation.

- The essence of market allocation: price mechanism.

- How to balance between efficiency represented by market allocation and control of externalities represented by urban planning and zoning.

Toward the end of this chapter, I propose how to reform the land tenure system in China.

SOCIAL STRUCTURE, ECONOMIC STRUCTURE, AND INCOME DISTRIBUTION

As mentioned above, China's growth rate since 1979 has been ranked among the highest for the longest period for almost any nation in modern history—a great achievement of China's open and reform policy. However, as shown in the next two sections, its income disparity, particularly its urban/rural income ratio, has become one of the worst in East Asia, and perhaps in the world.

The World Bank (1993) defines the real economic miracle as growth with equity. There is truth in this definition. Many countries have achieved high growth, but few have achieved good income distribution. Among those having achieved relatively equal income distribution, most found their economic growth stagnated. Few nations have achieved high growth and relatively equal income distribution at the same time. For these few, they truly deserve to be crowned as economic miracles.

To achieve this, it is necessary to keep the sectoral share in the total labor force (defined here as the social structure) close to its sectoral share in total GDP (defined here as the economic structure). In other words, the social structure should evolve closely and in the same direction as the economic structure (Wen 2013).

In China's context, the share of agriculture in the total labor force should follow the trend of a declining share of agriculture in total GDP. To achieve this, the rural population must find their way out of the agricultural sector as its share in total GDP falls.

Developed economies have already reached a very low farming share in GDP (2–5 percent) and a correspondingly low farming share in total population (2–9 percent). It took several hundred years for them to achieve both. The other East Asian economies accomplished this much faster, in roughly 30–40 years, starting from the early 1960s after a land reform to provide farmers an equal footing in land distribution in the early 1950s. The rights to free land trading and free rural-urban migrating enabled Japan, South Korea, and Taiwan to not only achieve high growth but also help prevent the worsening of their urban/rural income distributions. According to Oshima (1998, Figure 1), the values of the Gini coefficient in Japan, South Korea, and Taiwan never exceeded 0.4 during the period 1955–1995. Since then, their social structures have been evolving closely to the changes in their economic structure because without institutional barriers, farmers could freely trade their land and freely migrate to urban areas and to settle down there.

The Much-Worsened Income Distribution

However, Oshima (1998, Figure 1) shows that, in sharp contrast, China started with a relatively low Gini coefficient value of around 0.2 in the mid-1960s; this value rose significantly above 0.4 by the mid-1990s. Since then, the income distribution has worsened until recently. According to Wildau and Mitchell (2016), the value of the Gini coefficient in China rose to 0.49 in 2012.

Han, Zhao, and Zhang (2016) put China's income distribution inequality in a more global perspective. As Figure 6.1 shows, the value of China's Gini coefficient (0.481) was very close to that of the Latin American average (0.486), and significantly higher than that of several other continents.

In addition to high values of the Gini coefficient, the urban/rural ratio in China is also very high. Based on China's official data (*Xinhua* 2017), the urban/rural income ratio was 2.72 in 2016.[1] Using this ratio, one can easily see that the average income of people living in rural areas was only about 36.76 percent of the income of those living in urban areas. This ratio was once as high as 3.3:1 in 2013; obviously this indicator is now looking better.[2] However, in terms of income gap, the urban-rural income disparity is still worsening—it increased from CNY19,758 in 2015 to CNY21,253 in 2016 (*Xinhua* 2017).

WHY CAN ONLY ENDOGENOUS URBANIZATION BEST ACCOMMODATE RURAL POPULATION?

Urbanization provides the best channel of social mobility for the vast majority of the rural population in terms of their income and their

Figure 6.1 International Comparison of Gini Coefficient Values

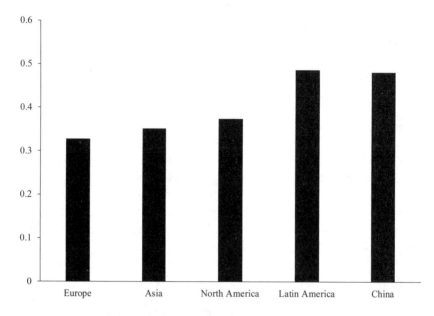

SOURCE: Han, Zhao, and Zhang (2016, Fig. 3.2).

upward movement along the social ladder. This is attributed to opportunities for greater specialization among these laborers, and to the ability to combine with the huge stock of capital and human capital agglomerated in urban areas.

When urbanization is endogenous—that is, driven by agglomeration effect, not simply by the government—then those who migrate to urban areas will be able to earn a higher income, and their children will have a better education than rural residents in general; otherwise, people will not choose to leave their native villages.

Figure 6.2 shows the determination of population size in an endogenously urbanizing city. The curve MB represents the marginal benefit of the agglomeration, and the curve MC represents the marginal cost of agglomeration, such as congestion, pollution, crime, and legal risks. The last one is conspicuously significant because of the insecure property rights and seriously distorted land and housing prices. The intersec-

Figure 6.2 The Agglomeration Effect of Urbanization and the Deadweight Loss

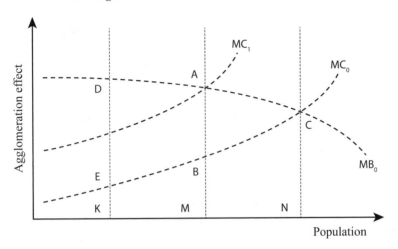

tion of the two curves C, or the corresponding point N on the horizontal axis, indicates the natural population size of the city. The space on its left, where the MB curve is still above the MC curve, implies that the net agglomeration is still positive, and the city can generate net gains by attracting additional migrants.

In other words, positive agglomeration effect can only be exhausted through trial and error by marginal migrants. To try out this population boundary of a city, rural residents must have the right to freely relocate themselves and to freely trade their land in case they decide to settle down in a city.

THE FIRST TRAP: HUKOU AND LOW SOCIAL MOBILITY

Two institutions stand out as the most important barriers for the rural population to legally share urban prosperity and to accumulate wealth on equal footing: the hukou system and the land tenure system.[3] China's hukou system has resulted in urbanization of land much faster than the growth of the rural population.

The hukou system, represented by line KD, artificially limits the size of urban population to OK (O refers to the origin of the graph). Therefore, population measured by KN is excluded from the benefit of urbanization. The triangle CDE measures the deadweight loss caused by the hukou system. As mentioned above, for income distribution between urban and rural areas not worsening, the social structure should evolve in the same direction as a nation's economic structure and at a similar pace.

China's agricultural share in its total GDP has fallen to less than 10 percent, representing a great achievement for China in its effort to develop its economy. However, given this rapid drop in its agricultural share in GDP, it is more urgent to reduce the share of its rural population in its total population. It is not a good sign to see that more than 60 percent of its total population is still holding rural hukou, and around 48 percent of its total population is still living in rural areas.

Migrant workers are forbidden to legally settle in urban areas, although they are legally allowed to work there temporarily, and their children—some 60 million—are left behind in rural areas. The lack of educational opportunities in rural areas dictates that most migrant children will have limited human capital and will have low social mobility and low incomes in the future. If this situation continues, the prospect for China to improve its urban-rural income distribution is severely clouded.

THE GOOD NEWS

The central government is gradually dismantling the hukou system. Although big cities will remain closed to most migrant workers, towns and small cities are urged to open up to rural migration. Only time will tell how effective and how soon China can ultimately eliminate the control over free migration and free settlement. It remains to be seen if the rural population in the Western region is allowed to freely settle in towns and small cities in China's prosperous coastal region. If such free migration and settlement between regions are allowed, the policy will represent a significant breakthrough.

THE SECOND TRAP—LAND TENURE SYSTEM

Compared with the hukou system, the land tenure system is an even bigger trap for the following reasons:

- It gives local governments either a legal basis or an excuse by misinterpreting Article 10 of China's Constitution to take rural land for urban development.

- It prevents the growth of a true land market by prohibiting all land trading except by the government. The government under this system becomes a monopsony in buying farmers' land and a monopoly in auctioning the leaseholds to developers. The land price is seriously distorted, either inflated or suppressed.

- The monopolized and seriously distorted land markets have almost totally ignored the strong demand of migrant workers for affordable housing thus far. Affordable houses have been supplied by suburban farmers, but they are illegal under the land system, frequently facing demolition risk, making the permanent settlement of migrant workers impossible.

In the absence of a true land market, the current land system is still allocating land through issuing land quotas to provinces and cities, a practice typically seen under the Central Planning System. However, these land quotas are not based on equilibrium land prices, hence, excess supply and rampant shortage coexist without an automatic correcting mechanism. On one side, ghost towns, idling apartment buildings, and deserted industrial parks are emerging everywhere, especially in China's vast inland, but in its coastal areas, housing prices are skyrocketing; on the other side, most of the 2.6 hundred million migrant workers are living in shelters, slums, ghettos, or urban villages, which are being bulldozed by the local governments, aggravating the shortage of affordable housing.

Clearly the current land tenure system has shifted upward the marginal cost of living in an urban area by making housing and rental prices prohibitively expensive in coastal areas where most migrant workers could find jobs. Figure 6.2 shows that when the marginal cost curve shifts up, the size of the city population reduces from point N to point A, causing another deadweight loss measured by triangle ABC.

In summary, the current land tenure system has failed to allocate both rural and urban land efficiently, and it has failed to convert rural land into urban land efficiently and fairly. The last point will be explained shortly.

THE IMPOSSIBILITY OF DEVELOPING A TRUE LAND MARKET UNDER THE CURRENT CONSTITUTION

Article 10 of China's Constitution makes it impossible to nurture a true land market. According to this article,

> land in the cities is owned by the State. Land in the rural and suburban areas is owned by collectives except for those portions which belong to the State as prescribed by law; house sites and privately farmed plots of cropland and hilly land are also owned by collectives.
>
> The State may, in the public interest and in accordance with law, expropriate or requisition land for its use and make compensation for the land expropriated or requisitioned.
>
> No organization or individual may appropriate, buy, sell or otherwise engage in the transfer of land by unlawful means. The right to the use of land may be transferred according to law. All organizations and individuals using land must ensure its rational use.

Why is it impossible to develop a real land market under such Constitutional stipulations? First, let's review the definition of what is a market economy. According to the *MIT Dictionary of Modern Economics* (Pearce 1992, p. 267), "An economic system in which decisions about the allocation of resources and production are made on the basis of prices generated by voluntary exchanges between producers, consumers, workers and owners of factors of production. Decision making in such an economy is decentralized—decisions are made independently by groups and individuals in the economy rather than by central planners. Market economies usually also involve a system of private ownership of the means of production—i.e., they are 'capitalist' or 'free enterprise' economies."

Here, voluntary exchanges are most crucial to a market economy. However, the collective land ownership observed in China is established on an involuntary basis. Rural collectives are not allowed to trade land among themselves, let alone the individual farmers. Even if a collective is totally inefficient or corrupt, or its leaders are abusive, members are not allowed to exit with their share of land to regroup a new collective on a truly voluntary basis. This means that collectives in China are compulsory against the market principle of voluntarism.

This system plays the function of permanently trapping those who want to leave their native village. They are not allowed to sell their land for market compensation. The rental market is underdeveloped and insecure because tenancy is not protected and leasing contracts are mostly verbal. Some peasants would rather keep their land vacant than return land to collectives or rent it out. This means that those who are determined to stay in the farming sector cannot steadily expand their land scales or significantly increase their incomes because of small-scale land operation. Because they do not own their land, they cannot use it as collateral when seeking financial services.

Therefore, the land tenure system in its current form is preventing the emergence of a real land market and consequently is preventing China's agriculture from being modernized and more efficient.

WHY IS EQUILIBRIUM LAND PRICE CRUCIAL?

In the absence of a true land market, land prices are not generated by the forces of supply and demand. Therefore,

- We do not know the opportunity cost of each piece of land in order to put it to the most valuable (efficient) use.

- We do not know how to fairly compensate those whose land is taken away by the government.

- We do not know what should be the fair base for property, housing, and capital gains taxes. Without tax revenues from land properties, governments at all localities will continue to be addicted to land financing.

- We do not know how to allocate land of different uses in the correct proportions, because such price information can only be generated through arbitrage among land of different uses in land markets.

- We do not know whether the decision on setting 1.8 billion mu of arable land as a red line is scientifically based.
- We do not know whether estate-based mortgages are overleveraged, leading to housing bubbles and financial crises.
- Urbanization cannot be an endogenous process and cannot sustain because of the distortion in land and housing prices. The service sector is doomed to be underdeveloped because of the prohibitively high rentals.
- Ghost towns are mushrooming everywhere, when hundreds of millions of migrant workers desperately need affordable housing in the urban areas where they are working and living. Unfortunately, the misallocation of land and housing forces them to live in slums, shelters, and urban villages.

FREE EXIT RIGHTS ARE THE KEY

Based on the discussion of the hukou and land systems above, we can see that it is urgent and necessary to thoroughly reform the two systems. In what follows, I want to focus on how to reform the current land system. To facilitate discussion, we divide all the land in China into three basic zoning categories conceptually in terms of their relationship to urbanization:

1) nonurban land—pure farmland and nonfarmland located far away from any urban areas, thus unlikely to be urbanized in the foreseeable future;

2) urban land—built-up land located in existing urban areas, thus fully urbanized;

3) suburban land—the farmland and nonfarmland located close to urban centers that is yet to be urbanized.

To nurture a true land market, the boundaries of all the plots must be clearly marked and recorded and their property rights registered before they can be traded at market without disputes. As a very encouraging development in this direction, local governments in China have been certifying land use rights of each farmer by delineating the borders of each plot and its legal users. Obviously, the completion of this task is conducive to the establishment of a true open and competitive land market.

All the land, however, is either owned by the state (all the urban land) or collectives (almost all the farmland, including the suburban land). Individual farmers and urban citizens are not allowed to trade land. As we mentioned above, the land market in its current form is monopsonistic because the state is the only legal buyer of land, and also monopolistic because the state is the only legal supplier of urban land, far from being a typical land market that is open to everyone on a competitive level.

To widen participation in a land market to make it open and competitive, it is necessary to allow all plots to be tradable and all the farmers to participate as sellers or buyers of land. For this reason, the exit rights must be returned to farmers. As mentioned earlier, the current collective land ownership was imposed on farmers in the 1950s without necessary consent from farmers. Such imposition was not only a violation of voluntarism, a principle allegedly cherished by the Chinese Communist Party, but it also led to rampant inefficiency and frequent power abuse. In the spirit of voluntarism, farmers should be given the choice to stay in their current collectives if they like them, to exit to form new collectives on their own initiatives, or to return to family-based farming, which is the prevailing form of farming in the rest of the world. In other words, land privatization should be permitted if the party truly respects initiatives from farmers themselves. In this sense, certifying and documenting all the plots, pushed by the party and government, are correct and necessary steps toward this direction.

Above I divided all the land into three basic zoning categories. Now I briefly examine how a true land market will affect each of them. The long-standing mismatches between demand for and supply of land in different categories under the current land system will gradually be corrected. First, in urban areas, trading land with different uses will generate the information required for adjusting zoning by observing the relative prices of industrial, residential, commercial, and infrastructural land. By gradually easing the restriction on arbitrage among land of different uses, efficiency in allocating the existing urban land can be significantly improved. The excess supply of certain types of land, such as land originally designated as industrial, will be corrected by its falling price, and the undersupplied land of another type, such as the land originally designated as residential, will be corrected by rising price.

Second, by allowing suburban farmland to enter the land market by farmers' own initiative without changing zoning categories, China can avoid the possible chaotic situation that resulted from zoning violations. At the same time, local governments are not allowed to requisition suburban land unless for the pursuit of public interest. This will immediately lead to the short supply of urban land and increased land prices where urban areas are growing. The increasing price sends a signal to zoning authorities to speed up converting suburban farmland into urban land. The suburban land market is crucially important because it connects urban and rural areas, unifying the whole nation's land market, and also helps determine the natural border between rural and urban areas.

Third, more efficient farmers now can expand the operation scale of their farms through acquiring land at land market, and larger and modern farms will emerge from such transactions. Those who want to permanently migrate to urban areas will get compensated when they sell their land.

As stated earlier, to avoid disorder in land and housing markets, neither sellers nor buyers of any type of land should be allowed to change the current zoning categories of their land for the time being unless they first obtain approvals from the government. Under this condition, free land trade will not trigger a collapse of the land and housing markets. The fear of a possible collapse of land and housing markets is a main source of government hesitation in land system reform, a serious concern often cited by those who are opposed to the market-oriented land reform as a main argument. To remove government's fear, the current zoning categories should be kept for a certain period. The planning and zoning office should gradually adjust zoning categories by designating more land in suburban areas as urban land if the land price there is rising, and designating less land as urban land in urban areas where the land price is declining.

To reduce manipulation and interference in the land market, the government should stop acquisitioning land from local farmers for nonpublic purposes, as Article 10 of China's Constitution stipulates. This means that the role of planning and zoning in China should be fundamentally reformed; its rise in market economies was, and is still, a necessary response to the increasing need to address market failure, represented by negative externalities and lack of public space due to urbanization (Wen 2014). However, in China, different from playing a complementary role in market allocation, as is seen in developed market economies, planning and zoning are a main remnant of its dismantled Central Planning System, and the government has been directly allocating land by arbitrarily determining land zoning and prohibiting non-state-owned land to enter land market with equal rights. It is worth noting that China's urban planning and zoning are selectively regulating market failures, depending on the type of land ownership, as the case of the urban village shows.

After establishing a true land market, the main target of planning and zoning should focus on filtering negative externalities and securing land of public use, not on filtering out the non-state-owned land. The thorny issue of urban villages and housing with few property rights will be resolved accordingly. Since they are either surrounded by or adjacent to urban areas, they should be part of urban land. Therefore, the local government has the same responsibilities to provide better planning and zoning regulation to all the urban villages and housing with few property rights, and better infrastructures such as sanitation, clean water, public toilets, schools, and clinics. In return, the owners in urban villages and owners of housing with few property rights have full obligation to pay all kinds of property taxes and capital gains taxes. If this proposal is accepted and enforced, the issue of urban village and housing with few property rights will be an issue of enforcing planning and zoning instead of an issue of discriminating against nonstate ownership.

Finally, the government should stop relying on land financing and instead levy property, housing, and capital gains taxes, in addition to issuing local public bonds to finance local infrastructure, using future land taxes to pay off. Land taxes are recurrent compared with one-time land financing. The latter will dry up sooner or later when urbanization nears an end.

CHINA IS AT A CROSSROADS

China's urban-rural income disparity is among the worst in the world. Historical experiences from developed nations and from China's

East Asian neighbors eloquently demonstrate that to reduce this disparity, China must rapidly reduce its rural population. Only when a nation's social structure matches its economic structure can it achieve the goal of narrowing its urban/rural income gap. However, not only does 48 percent of China's total population live in rural areas while its agriculture's share in total GDP is less than 10 percent, but also 2.6 hundred million migrant workers remain unsettled in urban areas because of the hukou system, and because of the prohibitively high housing prices as a result of the current land tenure system.

As Figure 6.2 shows, the hukou and land systems are causing two types of deadweight loss—if they can be eliminated, then China can easily accommodate hundreds of millions of migrant workers and their families in urban areas. To make its urbanization more efficient and inclusive, China should focus on urbanizing its rural population rather than its rural land. If China decides to nationalize all the urban land, as advocated by some, then it will lose its last chance to develop a land market. If China is serious about nurturing a true competitive land market, it needs to give farmers the exit rights from compulsory collective land ownership and legalize land trading as long as the land use is not changed by users themselves.

China should also unify its land market nationwide. To avoid permanently fragmenting its rural land market, it should not consolidate the exclusively community-based collective land ownership. China should also abolish its hukou system as soon as possible. Only when it implements these two reforms can the country accelerate the absorption of rural surplus labor. Such an endogenous urbanization will soon significantly improve its urban-rural income disparity, as the experiences from China's East Asian neighbors have demonstrated.

Notes

1. According to this official news agency, "Urban and rural per capita disposable income reached 33,616 yuan and 12,363 yuan in 2016, up 5.6 percent and 6.2 percent in real terms, respectively, according to the National Bureau of Statistics." Based on these two numbers, we can calculate the urban-rural income ratio (See *Xinhua* 2017).

2. According to the 2013 data released from the China State Statistical Bureau, in 2012 China's urban-rural income ratio reached its highest since 1978. In 2012, urban average income was 17,175 yuan, while it was 5,153 yuan in rural areas, and the urban-rural income ratio was 3.33:1, compared to 3.32:1 and 3.31:1 in 2007 and 2008, respectively. If we include the hidden benefits received by residents with formal urban hukou, this ratio could rise to 6:1. See http://wenda .so.com/q/1363044987065138 (in Chinese; accessed June 21, 2017).

3. In 1958, the Chinese government officially promulgated the family register system to control the movement of people between urban and rural areas. Individuals were broadly categorized as a rural or urban worker. A worker seeking to move from the country to urban areas to take up nonagricultural work would have to apply through the relevant bureaucracies. The number of workers allowed to make such moves was tightly controlled. Migrant workers would require six passes to work in provinces other than their own. People who worked outside their authorized domain or geographical area would not qualify for grain rations, employer-provided housing, or health care.

References

Han, Jin, Qingxia Zhao, and Mengnan Zhang. 2016. "China's Income Inequality in the Global Context." *Perspectives in Science* 7: 24–29. http://www .sciencedirect.com/science/article/pii/S2213020915000518#bbib0040 (accessed July 16, 2017).

Naughton, Barry, and Kellee S. Tsai. 2015. *State Capitalism, Institutional Adaptation, and the Chinese Miracle* (Comparative Perspectives in Business History). Cambridge: Cambridge University Press.

Oshima, Harry T. 1998. "Income Distribution Policies in East Asia." *Developing Economies* 36(4): 359–386.

Pearce, David W., ed. 1992. *The MIT Dictionary of Modern Economics*. 4th ed. Cambridge, MA: MIT Press.

Wen, Guanzhong James. 2013. "Introduction to the Special Issue on China's Three Agrarian Issues." *Modern China Studies* 20(2): 2–56.

———. 2014. "What Should Zoning Aim to Filter: Market Failure or Entry Rights of Non-State Owned Land? A Discussion with Mr. Chen Xiwen on

How to Dismantle the Urban-Rural Dual Structures." *Academic Monthly* 48(8): 5–17.

Wildau, Gabriel, and Tom Mitchell. 2016. "China Income Inequality among World's Worst." *Financial Times*, January 14. https://www.ft.com/content/3c521faa-baa6-11e5-a7cc-280dfe875e28 (accessed July 28, 2017).

World Bank. 1993. *The East Asian Miracle: Economic Growth and Public Policy*. World Bank Policy Research Report. New York: Oxford University Press.

Xinhua. 2017. "China's Personal Income Rises 6.3 Percent in 2016." January 20. http://news.xinhuanet.com/english/2017-01/20/c_135999545.htm (accessed July 17, 2017).

7

Trade, Migration, and Growth

Evidence from China

Xiaodong Zhu
University of Toronto

Citizens in rich countries such as the United States and those in the European Union have enjoyed two fundamental economic freedoms: free movement of goods and movement of people. This has not been the case, however, for citizens in many developing countries, where governments often impose significant restrictions on internal movements of both goods and people. Economists have argued that these restrictions create distortions that result in lower income and welfare for the citizens in these countries. Restrictions on free movement of goods shield inefficient producers from competition and therefore lower the average productivity of firms and raise the costs of goods faced by consumers. Restrictions on movement of people prevent workers from seeking more productive opportunities and households from moving to high-income regions, which leads to persistent labor misallocation and regional income inequality. Removing these restrictions can improve citizens' welfare in these countries by increasing product market competition and reducing labor misallocation, which leads to higher aggregate productivity.

In this chapter I use the period 2000–2005 in China as a case study of the benefits of reducing restrictions on movements of goods and people in an economy. In 2000, China had significant restrictions on internal trade, as well as severe restrictions on movement of people within the country because of a very stringent household registration system called *hukou*. Both restrictions were relaxed between 2000 and 2005. China also joined the World Trade Organization (WTO) at the end of 2001, which required China to reduce its international trade barriers, especially the import barriers.

During the same period, China's real GDP grew more than 11 percent per year. How much of the GDP growth can be attributed to the reductions in restrictions on movements of goods and people? I will provide a quantitative answer to this important question.

For background, I first discuss the state of the Chinese economy in year 2000 and some important changes that happened between 2000 and 2005. I focus my discussion on three aspects: 1) regional income inequality, 2) internal migration, and 3) trade.

SPATIAL DISTRIBUTION OF INCOMES AND INTERNAL MIGRATION

The cross-province differences in real income have been large in China. In 2000, the ratio of average real GDP per capita of the top five provinces to that of the bottom five was almost 4 to 1. Figure 7.1 plots the spatial distribution of real incomes across the Chinese provinces. The provinces of the coastal regions in the east generally had substantially higher levels of real income than provinces in the central and western regions.

Despite the large cross-province income differences, the percentage of workers who moved between provinces was very low because of a hukou registration system, which was introduced by the Chinese government in 1958 to control population mobility and urbanization. Under this system, each Chinese citizen is assigned a hukou (registration status), classified as "agricultural" (rural) or "nonagricultural" (urban) in a specific administrative unit that is at or lower than the county/city level. Approvals from local governments are needed for an individual to change the category (agricultural or nonagricultural) or location of hukou registration, and it is extremely difficult to obtain such approvals. Before the economic reform started in 1978, working outside one's hukou registration location/occupation category was prohibited. This prohibition was relaxed in the 1980s, and China started to have migrant workers who worked outside their hukou registration locations. However, prior to 2003 migrant workers were required to apply for a temporary residence permit, which was difficult to obtain. As a result, many migrant workers were without a permit and faced the dire consequence

Figure 7.1 Real GDP per Capita (relative to mean), 2000

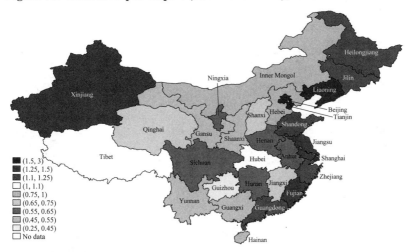

SOURCE: National Bureau of Statistics of China.

of being arrested and deported by the local authorities. Even with a temporary residence permit, migrant workers without local hukou had very limited access to local public services and faced much higher costs for health care and for their children's education. As the demand for migrant workers in manufacturing, construction, and labor-intensive service industries increased, many provinces, especially the coastal provinces, eliminated the requirement of a temporary residence permit for migrant workers, and by 2003 all provinces had eliminated the requirement. This policy change helped ease migration, but migrant workers still face the costs of having only very limited access to local public services. More importantly, migrant workers always face these costs as long as they do not have local hukou. Because of these costs, most migrant workers are young and without children, and their migration is temporary. In 2000, for example, 70 percent of migrant workers were without children, and 70 percent of them moved within the last four years. Most of them had agricultural hukou but were working in the nonagricultural sector.

As Table 7.1 shows, in 2000, there were 26.5 million migrant workers who worked outside the province of their hukou registration provinces. As the restrictions on migrant workers relaxed, the number

Table 7.1 Stock of Migrant Workers in China

	Interprovincial		Intraprovincial	
	2000	2005	2000	2005
Total stock (millions)	26.5	49.0	90.1	120.4
Share of total employment (%)	4.2	7.2	14.3	17.7

NOTE: Migrants are defined based on their hukou registration location. Interprovincial migrants are workers registered in another province from where they are employed. Intraprovincial migrants are workers registered in the same province where they are employed, but are either nonagricultural workers holding agricultural hukou or vice versa.
SOURCE: Author's calculations.

increased to 49 million in 2005. These are enormous numbers; however, they only represent 4.2 and 7.2 percent of China's total employment in 2000 and 2005, respectively. The majority of migrant workers in China are those who move within a province. The numbers of within-province migrant workers were around 90 million in 2000 and 120 million in 2005, representing 14.3 and 17.7 percent of China's total employment in 2000 and 2005, respectively.

INTERNAL AND EXTERNAL TRADE

It has been well documented that internal trade costs in China in the 1990s were high (Poncet 2005; Young 2000). It has also been documented that the degree of local market protection in a province was directly related to the size of the state sector in that province (Bai et al. 2004). Since 2000, these trade barriers have been reduced significantly. Some of the reduction was a result of the deliberate policy reforms undertaken by the government. For example, the state council under the then premier Zhu Rongji issued a directive in 2001 that prohibits local government from engaging in local market protections. More importantly, as a result of various state-owned enterprise reforms, the size of the state sector has declined significantly and consequently lowered local government incentives to engage in local market protections. Improved transport infrastructure and logistics also helped lower internal trade cost.

The province-level trade data, both between province pairs and internationally, are taken from the regional input-output tables for 2002 and 2007. Table 7.2 reports the aggregate bilateral flows between the eight regions and each other and the rest of the world. To ease comparisons, we normalize all flows by the importing region's total expenditures. In addition to the bilateral trade flows, we also report in the last column the share of a region's expenditures that are spent on goods from all other regions within China. A useful measure of a region's trade openness is the fraction of its expenditures allocated to its own producers—that is, its "home share." The diagonal elements in Table 7.2 provide these values for each region. Interior regions of China have a much higher home share than coastal regions. In 2002, the central region's home share is 0.88 compared to only 0.72 for the south coast and 0.63 for Beijing and Tianjin.

While regions in China generally import more from abroad than from any particular region within China, the total imports from the rest of China are still higher than imports from abroad for most of the regions. The Central Coast and South Coast regions are the exceptions. In 2002, their imports from abroad were significantly higher than imports from the rest of China; they also had substantial international exports.

TRADE AND MIGRATION COSTS IN CHINA

Tombe and Zhu (2015) use a structural model combined with the data on trade and migration flows to estimate costs of trade and migration. The model generates gravity equations that relate the trade flow between two regions to the real GDP of the two regions and the trade cost between the two regions, and the migration flow between two regions to the real incomes of the two regions and the cost of migration between two regions.

Trade flow between regions A and B = F(GDP of region A, GDP of region B, distance, *trade cost*)

Migration flow from regions A to B = G(income of region A, income of region B, distance, *migration cost*)

Table 7.2 Internal and External Trade Shares of China

Importer	Exporter									Total other prov.
	Northeast	Beijing/ Tianjin	North Coast	Central Coast	South Coast	Central Region	Northwest	Southwest	Abroad	
Year 2002										
Northeast	87.9	0.7	1.0	0.8	1.3	1.1	0.8	0.9	5.5	6.6
Beijing/Tianjin	3.9	63.4	9.4	3.0	2.6	3.3	1.4	1.2	11.9	24.8
North Coast	1.8	3.3	79.8	3.4	1.8	3.8	0.9	0.8	4.4	15.8
Central Coast	0.2	0.2	0.6	81.0	1.5	2.4	0.5	0.5	13.3	5.7
South Coast	0.5	0.4	0.5	2.6	72.3	1.9	0.4	1.5	19.8	7.9
Central Region	0.6	0.3	1.1	4.8	2.3	87.8	0.7	0.7	1.8	10.4
Northwest	2.0	0.8	2.1	3.3	4.5	3.6	77.4	3.8	2.6	20.0
Southwest	0.9	0.3	0.4	1.8	4.3	1.4	0.9	88.0	2.0	10.0
Abroad	0.0	0.0	0.0	0.1	0.2	0.0	0.0	0.0	99.6	–
Year 2007										
Northeast	78.7	2.0	2.0	0.9	2.7	1.0	1.4	0.9	10.4	10.9
Beijing/Tianjin	3.8	62.3	10.1	1.5	2.4	1.8	2.1	0.7	15.5	22.2
North Coast	2.1	5.8	76.8	1.5	1.5	3.7	2.3	0.8	5.5	17.7
Central Coast	1.1	0.7	1.4	76.8	1.8	4.8	1.7	0.9	10.8	12.4
South Coast	1.5	0.9	1.7	5.2	68.5	3.6	1.8	2.8	14.1	17.4
Central Region	1.7	1.4	4.5	4.9	4.0	73.0	2.9	1.8	5.9	21.1
Northwest	2.3	2.2	4.8	2.7	5.5	3.6	65.6	3.6	9.8	24.6
Southwest	1.6	1.2	1.7	1.7	8.4	1.9	3.2	73.8	6.6	19.6
Abroad	0.0	0.1	0.1	0.4	0.2	0.0	0.0	0.0	99.1	–

NOTE: The table displays the share of each importing region's total spending allocated to each source region. See Tombe and Zhu (2015, Appendix A) for the mapping of provinces to regions. The column "Total other prov." reports the total spending share of each importing region allocated to producers in other provinces of China. The diagonal elements (the "home share" of spending"), the share imported from abroad, and the share imported from other provinces will together sum to 100%.

SOURCE: Author's calculations.

With data on GDP, income, distance, and trade and migration flows, the trade and migration costs can be estimated as residuals.

Migration Costs

We measure the migration cost as a factor that deflates a migrant's real income so that she is indifferent between migrating or staying in her hukou location. The cost may vary across the sector-location pairs. For example, if the cost of migrating to a destination is 3, then an individual will migrate to the destination if and only if the real income in the destination is at least three times as high as the real income the individual can earn by staying at her hukou location. We summarize these costs, their changes, and the initial migration flows in Table 7.3. Overall, migration costs are largest for migrants switching both sectors and provinces, with an average initial cost of nearly 38. In contrast, switching sectors within one's home province incurs average migration costs of 2.9. When estimating the migration costs by migrant worker's age, the costs are much higher for older workers. These patterns of migration costs are consistent with our discussion earlier that the most important source of the migration costs is the lack of access to local public services at the migration destination. This is clearly more important for older migrant workers and workers who are farther away from their hukou location.

Table 7.3 also reports the change in average migration costs between 2000 and 2005 in the last column. Overall, migration costs declined to 84 percent of their initial level. Costs to switch provinces fell the most, from 32.6 to 19.8. Sectoral switches within a worker's home region also fell, from 2.9 to 2.4.

Trade Costs

The trade cost we estimate is a comprehensive measure of barriers to trade that includes tariffs, transportation costs, and other nontariff barriers, such as local protection policies. It is represented as an iceberg cost. For example, if the export cost is 3, then for one unit of good to reach the export destination, it will cost the exporter three units of goods. For a typical province in China in 2002, the average trade cost was 3 in agriculture and 2 in nonagriculture, and the magnitudes of

Table 7.3 Migration Rates and Average Costs, by Sector and Province

	Initial share of employment	Migration costs		
		Level in 2000	Level in 2005	Relative change
Agriculture to nonagriculture migration cost changes				
Overall	0.16	3.4	2.9	0.84
Within province	0.13	2.9	2.4	0.84
Between province	0.03	37.8	23.2	0.61
Between provinces migration cost changes				
Overall	0.04	32.6	19.8	0.61
Within agriculture	0.003	71.9	63.7	0.89
Within nonagriculture	0.01	21.3	12.4	0.58
Overall	0.174	3.6	3.0	0.84

NOTE: Displays migration-weighted harmonic means of migration costs in 2000 and 2005. We use initial (year 2000) weights to average the 2005 costs to ensure the displayed change reflects changes in costs and not migration patterns.
SOURCE: Author's calculations.

internal and external trade costs are similar. So, trade costs were quite high in 2002. Overall, we find that poor regions face the highest export costs—consistent with existing cross-country evidence.

Table 7.4 presents the relative change in the nonagricultural trade costs for eight regions in China between 2002 and 2007. Some notable patterns emerge. Within China, trade costs were largely decreasing, with trade-weighted change in trade costs within China of −11 percent. For trade between China and the world, the average change in trade costs was −8 percent. Poor regions such as Central, Northwest, and Southwest experienced much larger reductions in export costs than rich regions did. Also, the reductions in China's costs of importing from the rest of the world were much larger than the reductions in China's costs of exporting to the rest of the world. These numbers suggest that around the time when China joined the WTO, there were significant reductions in China's internal trade costs and import costs and only modest reductions in China's export costs.

Table 7.4 Percent Change in Trade Costs, 2002–2007

				Exporter					
Importer	North-east	Beijing/Tianjin	North Coast	Central Coast	South Coast	Central Region	North-west	South-west	World
Northeast		−11.8	−16.7	−23.5	−24.7	−23.0	−18.0	−18.5	−27.7
Beijing/Tianjin	−14.2		−15.0	−15.5	−13.8	−23.9	−25.7	−18.5	−26.9
North Coast	−5.7	−1.0		−1.0	−11.2	−20.7	−22.6	−20.7	−20.3
Central Coast	−16.4	−5.2	−4.5		−11.2	−15.9	−17.9	−12.4	−19.1
South Coast	−18.4	−4.0	−15.1	−12.0		−20.7	−24.7	−20.8	−10.6
Central Region	−6.6	−5.2	−15.1	−6.7	−11.2		−19.1	−16.8	−27.9
Northwest	−4.0	−10.6	−20.0	−12.0	−18.6	−21.9		−17.8	−37.8
Southwest	−3.8	−1.2	−17.5	−5.4	−13.8	−19.1	−17.2		−27.7
World	−3.8	−0.2	−6.5	−1.6	9.7	−21.0	−29.4	−18.5	

SOURCE: Author's calculations.

THE EFFECT OF MEASURED COSTS CHANGES

In Tombe and Zhu (2015) we use a general equilibrium model to quantify the effect of the changes in trade and migration costs. In the quantitative analysis, we fit the initial equilibrium of our model to the Chinese data in 2002 and then quantify the impacts on aggregate productivity and welfare of various changes in trade and migration costs. I summarize the main results here.

The Effect of Lower Trade Costs

Table 7.5 displays the change in trade and migration flows, aggregate productivity, and welfare, and various other outcomes as a result of the changes in trade costs. Changes in trade shares are expenditure-weighted average changes across all provinces and sectors. Lower internal trade costs, not surprisingly, decrease the amount of international trade as households and firms reorient their purchase decisions toward domestic suppliers. The share of expenditures allocated to producers in another province typically increases by over 9 percentage points, while the share allocated to international producers falls by almost 1 percentage point. Lower external trade costs reveal the opposite pattern. In both cases, home shares fall.

Table 7.5 Effects of Trade Cost Changes

	Percentage point change in		Migrant stock (%)			
	Internal trade	External trade	Within province	Between province	Real GDP (%)	Aggregate welfare (%)
Internal trade	9.2	−0.7	0.8	−2.0	10.7	10.7
External trade	−0.7	3.9	1.8	2.4	3.8	2.6
All trade	8.2	2.9	2.5	0.3	14.4	13.2

NOTE: Displays aggregate response to various trade cost changes. All use trade cost changes as measured. The migrant stock is the number of workers living outside their hukou registration location or sector.
SOURCE: Author's calculations.

In terms of migration, improved internal trade costs actually resulted in fewer workers living outside their home province. The total stock of migrants declined by over 2 percent (equivalent to approximately 0.5 million workers). Intuitively, declining internal trade costs disproportionately lower goods prices in poor, interior regions. This increase in real income means that fewer workers living in other provinces were willing to continue to do so. On the other hand, a greater fraction of workers switched sectors within their home province. With lower international trade costs, richer coastal regions disproportionately benefit, so more workers relocate there in addition to more workers switching sectors within their home province.

The change in income, goods and land prices, and workers' location decisions all have implications for aggregate welfare. We report the change in welfare and productivity (aggregate real GDP) in the last columns of Table 7.5. In response to lower internal trade costs, aggregate welfare dramatically increased by nearly 11 percent. In contrast, external trade cost reductions resulted in a much smaller gain of only 3.1 percent. As in our earlier analysis, internal trade costs reductions appear to be significantly more important for aggregate outcomes. The differential impacts are not due to any significant differences in the magnitude of cost reductions. The main reason for the larger welfare gains from internal cost reductions is that most provinces allocate a larger fraction of their spending to goods from other provinces than from abroad.

The Effect of Lower Migration Costs

Trade liberalization accounts for only a limited amount of migration. Not surprisingly, lower migration costs lead to substantially more workers living outside their home province-sector. As before, we simulate the effect of lower migration cost changes and report the effects in Table 7.6.

The stock of migrants increases dramatically when the cost of migration declines as measured. The number of interprovincial migrants increases by more than 80 percent. Within provinces, there are also substantial moves from agriculture to nonagriculture. The stock of workers with agricultural hukou that have nonagricultural employment within their home province increases by nearly 15 percent. Clearly, the measured changes in migration costs are extremely important determinants of worker location decisions. The large flows are also beneficial for China as a whole; real GDP and welfare rise 4.8 and 8.5 percent, respectively. Changes that facilitate the movement of workers from agriculture to nonagriculture sectors, whether within or between provinces, account for most of the increases in aggregate GDP and welfare.

While migration flows and real incomes respond greatly to the changes in migration costs, the effect on aggregate trade flows is muted. International and internal trade shares increase by only 0.2 and 0.1 percentage points, respectively.

Table 7.6 Effects of Various Migration Cost Changes

	Percentage point change		Migrant stock			
	Internal trade	External trade	Within province (%)	Between province (%)	Real GDP (%)	Aggregate welfare (%)
All	0.1	0.2	14.5	82.4	4.8	8.5
Agriculture to nonagriculture migration cost changes						
Overall	0.1	0.1	15.3	54.0	4.4	7.2
Within province	0.0	−0.1	22.8	−9.6	2.0	4.8
Between province	0.1	0.2	−7.0	71.0	2.9	2.7

NOTE: Displays aggregate response to various migration cost changes. All use migration cost changes as measured. The migrant stock is the number of workers living outside their hook registration location or sector.
SOURCE: Author's calculations.

Decomposing China's Growth between 2000 and 2005

While the results above show that the reductions in trade and migration costs have a large effect on the aggregate GDP growth, they cannot account for all the observed growth in China between 2000 and 2005. Other factors, such as technology improvements and reforms within each province and sector may also contribute to the aggregate GDP growth during that period. In Tombe and Zhu (2015), we summarize the contribution of these factors by a residual productivity growth term for each province and sector so that the combination of the productivity growth and the measured changes in trade and migration costs can generate a GDP growth rate in our quantitative model that matches the actual GDP growth rate in that province and sector. By construction, the quantitative model with the measured cost changes and the implied residual productivity growth also matches the aggregate GDP growth exactly. The model can then be used to decompose China's overall growth into one of four components: productivity growth, lower internal trade costs, lower international trade costs, and lower internal migration costs. The result of the decomposition is reported in Table 7.7.

Overall, reductions in trade and migration frictions account for about one-third of China's overall growth. Reductions in internal trade and migration costs contribute roughly one quarter (15.3 percent of the 57.1 percent). In stark contrast, international trade cost reductions account for only 7 percent of the overall growth (4.2 percent of the 57.1 percent).

Potential Gains from Further Reform

Our decomposition shows that reductions in trade and migration frictions and the resulting reduction in misallocation of labor played a major role in China's growth between 2000 and 2005. How much additional scope is there for further reductions in trade and migration costs? In Tombe and Zhu (2015), we use the quantitative model to evaluate the effect of two potential reforms: 1) lowering the internal trade costs to the average level observed in Canada, and 2) lowering the internal migration costs so that the average interprovincial migration rate in China is the same as the interstate migration rate in the United States. The results are reported in Table 7.8 and show that China's real GDP and welfare could increase by a further 10.9 percent and 11.8 percent

Table 7.7 Decomposing China's Overall Real GDP Growth

	Marginal effects	
	Real GDP growth (%)	Share of growth
Overall (all changes)	57.1	—
Productivity changes	37.9	0.66
Internal trade cost changes	9.7	0.17
External trade cost changes	4.2	0.07
Migration cost changes	5.6	0.10

NOTE: Decomposes the change in real GDP into contribution from productivity, internal trade cost changes, external trade cost changes, and migration cost changes.
SOURCE: Author's calculations.

Table 7.8 Potential Gains of Further Trade and Migration Liberalization

	Relative to 2005	
	Change in Real GDP (%)	Aggregate welfare (%)
Average internal trade costs as in Canada	10.9	11.8
Between-province migration as in U.S.	22.8	15.0
Both changes together	37.0	30.5

NOTE: Reports the change in real GDP and welfare that result from changing China's internal trade and migration costs such that average internal costs equal Canada's (by sector) or such that the between-province migration flows match the U.S. Percentage changes are expressed relative to the Chinese economy in 2005.
SOURCE: Author's calculations.

if average internal trade costs fell to Canada's level, and an additional 22.8 percent and 15 percent if the average migration rate in China was the same as that in the United States. The scope for and gains from further policy reforms are therefore large. Both changes together would deliver real GDP gains of 37 percent and welfare gains of nearly 31 percent.

CONCLUSION

China experienced rapid GDP growth between 2000 and 2005, and many believe it is because of the external trade liberalization associated with China's joining the WTO in 2001. This resulted in export expansion supported by a large increase in the supply of cheap migrant workers, hence the growth. Internal policy reforms undertaken by the Chinese government during the same period have not received as much attention. However, their contribution to China's growth during that period is much more important than the contribution of the external trade liberalization. Reductions in internal trade and migration costs account for 27 percent of the aggregate GDP growth in China between 2000 and 2005. In contrast, reductions in external trade costs account for only 7 percent of the aggregate GDP growth during the same period. Despite the reductions, internal trade and migration costs in China are still much higher than those in developed countries such as Canada and the United States. Further reforms that lower these costs to developed country levels could yield substantial increases in China's aggregate GDP and welfare in the future.

Note

This chapter is largely based on my joint paper with Trevor Tombe (Tombe and Zhu 2015). I thank the Department of Economics at Western Michigan University for inviting me to present this paper at the 2015–2016 Werner Sichel Lecture Series.

The data on regional income are constructed based on the GDP and employment series provided by Brandt, Tombe, and Zhu (2013); the data on trade are from the Inter-Province Input-Output table provided by Li (2010) and the Inter-Regional Input-Output table provided by Zhang and Qi (2012); and the data on migration are from the 1 percent sample of the 2000 China Population Census and the 20 percent sample of the China 2005 1 Percent Population Survey.

There is no regional input-output table for 2000 in China, so we use trade shares from the 2002 China Regional Input-Output Tables to approximate trade shares in 2000.

References

Bai, Chong-en, Yingjuan Du, Zhigang Tao, and Sarah Tong. 2004. "Local Protectionism and Regional Specialization: Evidence from China's Industries." *Journal of International Economics* 63(2): 397–417.

Brandt, Loren, Trevor Tombe, and Xiadong Zhu. 2013. "Factor Market Distortions across Time, Space, and Sectors in China." *Review of Economic Dynamics* 16(1): 39–58.

Li, Shantong. 2010. *Nian Zhongguo Diqu Kuozhan Touru Chanchubiao (2002 China Extended Regional Input-Output Tables)*. Beijing: Economic Science Press.

Poncet, Sandra. 2005. "A Fragmented China: Measure and Determinants of Chinese Domestic Market Disintegration." *Review of International Economics* 13(3): 409–430.

Tombe, Trevor, and Xiaodong Zhu. 2015. "Trade, Migration and Productivity: A Quantitative Analysis of China." Working paper. Toronto, Ontario: University of Toronto.

Young, Alwyn. 2000. "The Razor's Edge: Distortions and Incremental Reform in the People's Republic of China." *Quarterly Journal of Economics* 115(4): 1091–1135.

Zhang, Yaxiong, and Shuchang Qi. 2012. *2002, 2007 Nian Zhongguo Qiqujian Touru Chanchubiao (2002 and 2007 China Inter-Regional Input-Output Tables)*. Beijing: China Statistical Press.

Authors

Wei-Chiao Huang is a professor of economics at Western Michigan University.

Yang Liang is a PhD candidate in the Department of Economics at Syracuse University.

Mary E. Lovely is a professor of economics at Syracuse University.

Barry Naughton is Sokwanlok Professor at the School of Global Policy and Strategy (GPS) of the University of California, San Diego.

Murray Scot Tanner is a senior research scientist at CNA Corporation.

Guanzhong James Wen is a professor emeritus of economics and international studies at Trinity College.

Wing Thye Woo is a professor of economics at University of California, Davis, and Sunway University.

Huizhong Zhou is a professor of economics at Western Michigan University.

Xiaodong Zhu is a professor of economics at the University of Toronto.

Index

Note: The italic letters *f, n,* or *t* following a page number indicate a figure, note, or table, respectively, on that page. Double letters mean more than one such consecutive item on a single page.

Afghanistan, relations with, 16, 21–22
Africa
  income inequality in, 54
  See also specific countries in, e.g.,
    Nigeria
Agricultural sector
  GDP and rural populations in, 108–
    109, 112, 120
  hukou and, 124, 125
  modernization of, delayed by land
    tenure, 115
Air pollution
  economic development and, 65–66,
    76*n*24
  effect of, on human populations, 69,
    70
Annual Survey of Industrial Production
  (ASIP), microdata provided by, 8,
    84, 86, 87, 93*t,* 94, 101
Antiterrorism, 3, 19, 24
Arab Spring uprisings, 22
Arctic region, strategic communication
  lines with, 16
ASEAN. *See* Association of Southeast
  Asian Nations
Asia
  Gini coefficients in, 53–54, 55*t,*
    75*n*12, 108–109, 110*f*
  See also regional areas, i.e., Central
    Asia; East Asia; Eurasia;
    Southeast Asia
Asian brown cloud, 69
Asian Development Bank, 1, 54, 55*t*
Asian Infrastructure Investment Bank, as
  rival, 1
Asian-Pacific nations, U.S. allies among,
  3, 18, 21, 72
ASIP microdata. *See* Annual Survey of
  Industrial Production

Association of Southeast Asian Nations
  (ASEAN)
  as U.S. Cold War allies, 72
  See also specific members in, i.e.,
    Indonesia; Malaysia; Philippines,
    The; Singapore; Thailand
Australia as U.S. ally, 23
Authoritarianism, 22, 33, 41

Bangladesh, 68
  offshoring Chinese production to, 4, 28
Brazil, leadership by, 71, 72
Burma, U.S. policy toward, 22

Canada
  social safety nets in, 58, 59*t*
  trade and migration in, compared,
    134–136, 135*t*
Capitalism, 47
  degrees of, 44, 59, 75*n*2, 76*n*17
  investment-motivated savings and,
    64, 76*n*23
  market-oriented economies as, 13, 36,
    39, 41, 50
  private sector involvement in, 7, 8–9,
    32, 114
Central Asia, China's strategic relations
  with, 16
Child laborers, agency failure to protect,
  8, 51–52, 75*n*11
China
  central planning in, 113, 116, 118–119
  distribution of workers in, and
    globalization, 58, 59*t,* 72
  economic failure possibilities in, 4–6,
    7–8, 29, 43–77
    (*see also* Income inequality)
  expanding economy of, and
    consequences, 1, 4, 12, 13, 62–65

China, *cont.*
family registration system in
(*see* Hukou system)
governance problems in, 2–3, 7–8,
18–20, 52
key security interests of, 2, 16–18
land tenure system in, 10, 11, 108,
113–114
military potential of, 1, 17, 24
minority populations of, 16, 23
provincial issues in, 45, 56, 125–126,
126*t*, 132
(*see also specific provinces, i.e.,*
Henan Province; Jiangsu Province;
Shanxi Province)
China. Food and Drug Safety Agency,
bribery and dereliction of, 7–8, 51
China. Ministry of Finance
investment companies proposed by,
vs. SASAC, 38–39
Lou Jiwei and, 34–35
China. Ministry of Public Security, 52,
75*n*11
China. Ministry of Water Resources,
erosion control by, 67
China. National Bureau of Statistics
(NBS)
ASIP data provided by, 8, 84, 86, 87,
93*t*, 94, 101
ownership classification assigned by,
85, 87–88, 102
China. State Environmental Protection
Agency, 70–71
China law and legislation, 20, 52, 85
hukou system, 10–11, 121*n*3
land ownership, 11, 113–114
China Sea
East, protecting China's security
interests in, 16, 17
South, China's expansion and tension
in, 1, 3, 15, 21
China Securities Finance Corporation,
stock market bubble bailout of, 6,
36
Chinese Communist Party (CPC), 52
capitalist-orientation and, 64, 76*n*17

Central Committees of, 45, 55, 71,
96–97, 103
congresses of, 13, 85
principles of, 22, 65, 117
protecting rule by, among key
security interests, 2, 16
shift from economic construction to
social harmony by, 45, 55–56, 74,
75*n*14, 95
Xi Jinping and, 13, 15, 39
Chinese government agencies
U.S. advantage in strengthening, 20
See also specifics, e.g., China. Food
and Drug Safety Agency
Chinese People's Public Security
University, lecture by U.S. cabinet
official at, 18
Christensen, Dr. Tom, China's power
status and, 1, 15
Climate change
economic development and, 65, 69
as environment disaster causing social
unrest, 8, 46
rainfall in, 67, 69, 76–77*n*30
Columbia, income inequality in, 55*t*
Communist Party of China. *See* Chinese
Communist Party (CPC)
Company Law (1994), restructuring in,
85
Competition, 28, 95, 120
U.S.-China issues of, 2, 15, 22, 24,
44, 56, 123
wages and, 57, 60
Consumers
compromised safety of, as dereliction
of government agency duty, 8,
51–52
costs for, 123, 125
income of, 102–103
Cooperation, U.S.-China issues of, 3, 15,
18, 24
Corporations
conversion of SOEs to, as reform, 39,
85, 97–98
stock market bubble bailout of, 6, 36

Corruption
    bribery in, 51–52
    crack down on, and domestic politics,
        4, 13, 32–33, 52
    as government software failure
        causing social unrest, 7–8, 46
    power abuse as, 52, 117
Côte d'Ivoire, income inequality in, 55*t*
Counterpiracy, 3, 24
CPC. *See* Chinese Communist Party
Criminal Law, human trafficking in, 52
Cultural Revolution, pre-1978 in China,
    28
Currency
    rigged, and U.S. competition, 57, 65
    RMB, 35, 86
    yuan as, for average urban/rural
        incomes, 109, 121*n*2
Cyber security
    military potential of, interests, 2, 15
    uses and abuses of, 17, 20

Dalai Lama, Tibetan rights and, 23
Debt
    accumulation of, as percent of GDP in
        China, 4, 30–31, 31*f*, 48–50, 49*n*6
    restructuring of local government, as
        reform, 5, 34–35
    SOB solvency and, 7, 43, 74*n*1, 75*n*7
Deng Xiaoping, collegial enlightened
    dictatorship under, 32, 59, 76*n*17
Diplomacy, U.S.-China relations and,
    1–3, 15
Disaster relief
    environmental, and power supply
        failure, 7, 8, 46
    as nontraditional security interest, 3,
        24
Domestic politics, 13
    CPC leadership in, and sustainability,
        2, 16, 45
    cronyism in, and government reform,
        44, 75*n*2
    foreign policy affected by, 3–4
    reform of, 4, 52, 56
    stock markets affected by, 5–6, 37

Dragon vs. Eagle (Huang and Zhou),
    market reforms and U.S.-China
    relations, 13
Drugs, substandard, as dereliction of
    safety agency duty, 8, 51

East Asia, 24
    beyond, and extended key Chinese
        security interests, 2, 16–18
    GDP and rural populations in, 108–109
    income inequality in, 10, 120
East China Sea, protecting Chinese
    interests in, 16, 17
Economic growth, 4, 45
    1978–2016 rates of, in China, 27–28,
        107
    2000–2005, and its decomposition,
        124, 134, 135*t*
    hardware failure in, with fiscal crisis,
        7, 43, 46, 47–50
    market-oriented reforms and, 13, 36,
        39, 134–136, 135*t*
    movement of goods and people in,
        11–13
    sustained technological and, among
        key security interests, 2, 16
    Xi Jinping vision of, 4, 5–6, 13
Economic growth, major threats to
    China's, 43–82
    causes of trade protection against
        China, 57–61
    conclusion, 71–74
    defects in the Chinese economy, 62–65
    defects in the U.S. economy, 57–61
    environmental collapse, 65–71
    hardware failure, 46, 47–50
    pessimism, 43–44, 74*n*1, 75*nn*2–3
    power supply failures, 46, 47, 56–57,
        58–61, 73–74
    rough road to prosperity, 44–57
    software failure, 46, 47, 50–56, 73–74
Economic reforms, 70
    debt restructuring, 5, 31, 34–35
    directed by LSG, 5, 6
    market-oriented, 13, 36, 39, 41, 134–
        136, 135*t*

Economic reforms, *cont.*
    possible failure of, 4–6, 27
        (*see also* Xi Jinping economic
        reform model)
    post failure of, and new initiative,
        40–41
    SOEs, 6, 8–9, 37–39
    stock markets in, 5–6, 36–37
Economic sustainability
    global environmental problems and,
        69–71
    political viability linked to, 47, 74,
        75n5
    profitability and, 91–92
Economic System and Ecological
    Civilization Specialized Group,
    responsibilities of, 33
Education, 54, 64
    access to, for urban *vs.* rural children,
        10, 63, 110, 1121
Employment
    migrant workers and, 125–126, 126t,
        132t, 133t
    offshoring and, 4, 28
Energy security
    burning fuels and, 69, 70, 73
    maintaining, with access to petroleum
        and natural gas, 16, 20
    power supply failure and trade
        conflicts in, 8, 56–57
Environmental collapse, 45
    air pollution in, 65–66, 76n24
    desertification as, 66–67, 70, 76n28
    power supply failure as, 8, 47, 48,
        56–57
    prevention of, 69–71, 73
    water shortage among, 66–71
Environmental problems, foreign NGOs
    and, 20
Equity markets. *See* Stock markets
EU. *See* European Union
Eurasia, collapse of Leninism in, 22
European Union (EU), 61, 123
    fiscal targets for members to meet,
        48–49
    as G4 member, 71, 72

income inequality in, 54, 110f
social safety nets in
    (*see under specific members,*
    i.e., France; Germany; Italy;
    United Kingdom)
trade conflicts with China, 56–57

Farmers, 108, 117
    exit rights of, from rural collectives,
        12, 115, 116–119
    savings rates and, 76n22, 107
Financial markets
    bailouts in, 6, 35, 43
    pooled risk and insurance in, 64, 65
    reform goals for, 5, 6, 20, 41, 65, 119
Fiscal crisis, as hardware failure in
    economic growth, 7, 30, 46, 47–50
Food, tainted, 8, 51
Foreign investment, 7, 17, 43
    Chinese stock market and, 36, 37
    unpredictable government policy and,
        6, 37
Foreign policy, 1, 3–4
France, social safety nets in, 58, 59t
Free trade
    benefits of, 71, 123, 134–136, 135t
    exchanging land in, manner, 111, 118
    U.S. doubts about, 71–72
Freedom of speech
    CPC pledge on, 55, 75n14
    suppression of, 4, 13, 20, 22, 51, 75n10

GATT. *See* General Agreement of Tariffs
    and Trade
GDP. *See* Gross Domestic Product
General Agreement of Tariffs and Trade
    (GATT), free trade regime of, 71
Germany, social safety nets in, 58, 59t
Globalization, 17, 30, 57
    distribution of workers and, 58–59,
        59t, 60, 72
    wage rates and, 60, 61, 76n19
Governance problems
    bureaucratic deficiencies in
        implementing agreements, 2, 15,
        18–20

Governance problems, *cont.*
China and U.S., compared, 11, 24
cronyism as, 44, 75*n*2
dereliction of duty by agency
officials, 51–52, 75*nn*8–11
software failure in, with social
disorders, 7–8, 46, 50–56,
75*nn*23–24
Government investments, 16, 64
infrastructure and, 28, 67–68, 69
profits and, 102–103
savings and, 62–65, 76*n*23
Government reforms, 5, 70
2013 Third Plenum Resolution as, by
Xi Jinping, 4, 6, 27, 33
attempted, of SOE, 6, 8–9
half-finished, as "trapped transition,"
44, 75*n*2
trade and migration gains from, 134–
136, 135*t*
Green growth policy, as economic
reform, 70
Gross Domestic Product (GDP), 45
China, compared to other nations, 44,
75*n*4, 108–109
contribution of trade and migration
costs to, 134, 135*tt*
debt accumulation as percent of, in
China, 4, 30–31, 31*f,* 48–50, 49*n*6
migration flows and, 12–13, 124, 133
percent of, 48, 63

Health care, 54, 70
insurance for, 64, 65
provision of, for urban *vs.* rural
workers, 10, 63
Heckscher-Ohlin model, world labor
force and, 60
Henan Province
dams in, and population
displacements, 68, 77*n*31
forced labor in, 51–52
Historical grievances, obstacles and
tensions as, 21, 22, 23–24
Hong Kong, foreign capital from, 86,
103*n*2

Hong Kong–Shanghai Capital Connect,
foreign investment and stock
market reform via, 36, 37
Horn of Africa, strategic communication
lines with, 16
Households, 74*n*1, 123
Housing, 64, 116, 118
price of, 111*f,* 113, 120
provision of, for urban *vs.* rural
workers, 10, 63–64
Hu Jintao, President
firm's state affiliation under, 97–98
Hu-Wen leadership under, 45–46, 56
reforms and, 32, 56, 84, 95, 103*n*1
Hukou system
dismantling of, 12, 13, 112, 120
exclusive urbanization and, 107,
111–112
family registration in, and suppressed
rural migration, 10, 121*n*3, 124–
125
restrictions of, being lifted, 11, 112,
123, 132*t*
Human capital
agglomerated, in urban areas, 110–111
job opportunities and, 54, 73
limited, and future social mobility and
income, 112
Human rights, 18, 21–22
Human trafficking, persistence of, 52,
75*nn*10–11
Humanitarian assistance, as
nontraditional security interest, 3,
24

ICT. *See* Information and
communications technology
Immigration. *See* Migration, cross-
country
Income, 61
distribution of, and migration, 124–
126, 125*f*
expectations of, 74, 110
middle- or high-, and institutional
barriers, 107, 123
See also types of, Salaries; Wages

Income inequality
    China's, compared, 10, 54, 55*t*
    Gini coefficients and, 53–54, 55*t*,
        75*n*12, 109, 110*f*
    poverty and, in social stability, 52–56
    regional, and changes in Chinese
        economy, 124, 125*f*, 127, 128*t*,
        130, 131*t*, 137
    rural/urban disparity and, 10–11, 107,
        109, 119–120, 121*nn*1–2
India, 55*t*, 59
    China's strategic relations with, 16,
        68, 69
    distribution of workers in, and
        globalization, 58, 59*t*, 60, 72
    leadership by, 44, 71, 75*n*2
    U.S. relations with, 18, 23
    wages in, 60, 76*n*18
Indian Ocean region, access to petroleum
    and natural gas through, 16
Indonesia, 55*t*
    fuel prices in, and presidential
        viability, 47, 75*n*5
    U.S. relations with, 23, 72
Industrial sector, 28, 83
    production and revenue data from, 86,
        107
    SOE reform and, 85, 88–91, 90*f*
    state control in, 87–89, 88*f*, 90*f*, 102
    worker protection in, 8, 75*n*11
Information and communications
    technology (ICT), wages and, 60,
    76*n*19
Infrastructure, 119
    government investment in, 28, 67–68,
        69
Insurance, as safety net, 61, 64
Intellectual property, 17, 20
International problem-solving
    global environmental management
        and, 70, 73
    local and state officials undermining
        national efforts at, 2–3, 18–20
International relations
    communist impact on countries
        worldwide, 22–23, 73

    power transition theory in, and
        strategic trust, 21–22
Iran, relations with, 16, 20
Italy, social safety nets in, 58, 59*t*

Japan, 5, 55*t*, 64, 70
    China expansion and conflict with, 1,
        23
    economic growth in, 4, 28, 29, 31–33
    GDP of, compared to China, 13,
        108–109
    social safety nets in, 58, 59*t*
    U.S. relations with, 18, 23–24, 72
    worker age in, compared to China,
        29–30
Jiang Zemin, collegial enlightened
    dictatorship under, 32, 44
Jiangsu Province, municipal bonds and
    interest rates in, 35
Job creation, 43, 54, 74*n*1
Job opportunities
    coastal areas with, 113, 124
    human capital and, 54, 73
    migrant workers and, 123, 125
Job tenure, globalization and, 58, 59*t*, 61
Johnson, Homeland Security Secretary
    Jeh, 18

Korea, 5, 70
    economic growth rate in, compared to
        China, 28, 31–33
    labor costs change in, and economic
        growth, 4, 29
    worker age in, compared to China,
        29–30
    See also North Korea; South Korea

Labor classification, assigned
    geographical domain and, 10
Labor costs, change in, 4, 28–29, 58, 61
Labor force. *See* Workers
Labor productivity
    firms with low, and SOEs, 9, 98
    offshore, compared to China, 4, 28
Land markets
    development of, prevented by land

tenure system, 113, 114–115, 120
price mechanisms and efficiencies in,
    107, 115–116
rights to free land distribution and
    trading in, 108–109
zoning categories for, and
    urbanization, 116, 117–118
Land ownership, 116
compulsory by collectives or State,
    11, 107, 114, 117
State acquisition of, for nonpublic
    purposes, 118–119
Land tenure system, 113–114
as barrier, 111, 114–115, 120
farmland conversion to industrial
    parks, 55, 113
reform of, in China, 10, 11, 75n14,
    108, 116–119
Land use rights, 116–117, 120
Latin America
income inequality in, 54, 109, 110f
    See also specific countries in, e.g.,
    Brazil
Leadership small group (LSG)
economic reforms directed by, vs.
    formerly by premier of State
    Council, 5, 33
managers' salaries limited by, 6, 37
specialized subgroups and delegated
    authority of, 6, 33, 38
Legacy burdens, state sector, 94–95, 98,
    99t
Leninism, aspects of, and China's
    international relations, 22–23
Levin, Rep. Sander, China trade and, 57
Li Keqiang, stock market bubble bailout
    by, 6, 36–37
Light Center for Chinese Studies, as
    lecture series sponsor, 25n1
Liu He, implementation of Xi's policy
    preferences by, 33
Local government
debt accumulation by, as percent of
    GDP, 4, 30–31, 31f
removing influence of, 7, 126

resources of, and undermine national
    efforts at international problem-
    solving, 2–3
restructuring of debt accumulated by,
    as reform, 5, 31, 34–35
rural land taken by, for urban
    development, 11, 113
Lou Jiwei, local debt restructuring laid
    out by, 34
LSG. See Leadership small group

Macao, foreign capital from, 86, 103n2
Malaysia, 16, 23, 72
Mandelson, Peter, EU trade and, 57
Manufacturing sector. See Industrial
    sector
Mao Zedong, 65, 67–68
Maritime security interests, protection of
    China's, 16
Market-oriented economies
capitalism in, 13, 36, 39, 41, 50
reforms to achieve economic growth
    with, 13, 36, 39, 76n16, 114,
    134–136, 135t
voluntarism in, 114–115
Medical care. See Health care
MFN (Most-favored-nation) status, 43
Migrant workers
employment of, 75n11, 125–126,
    126t, 132t, 133t
hukou and, 112, 120, 121n3, 124–
    125, 126t
permanent settlement of, 113, 116
wages of, over time, 29f, 65, 107
Migration
costs of, 12–13, 127–129, 130t, 133,
    133t, 136, 137
cross-country, 28, 29f, 61, 76n20
economic benefits and, 11–12, 123,
    133
rural, and hukou system, 10–11, 12,
    112
social mobility and, 109–110
Military potential, 17
naval modernization and development,
    1, 17–18, 24

Military potential, cont.
  reconnaissance flights near national
    borders, 3, 21
  space and cyber security interests, 2,
    15
Mining industry, worker protection in, 8,
  75n11
Most-favored-nation (MFN) status, WTO
  membership and, 43
Municipal bonds, transforming capped
  debt into, 5, 34–35, 40

National unity, 2, 16, 33
NBS. See China. National Bureau of
  Statistics
Nepal, income inequality in, 54, 55t
NGOs (Nongovernmental organizations),
  20
Nigeria, income inequality in, 55t
Nongovernmental organizations (NGOs),
  management of foreign, 20
Nonperforming loans (NPL)
  banking crisis with, as hardware
    failure, 46–47, 64
  evolution of debt-to-GDP ratio and,
    48–50
North America, Gini coefficients in, 110f
North Korea, nuclear and missile activity
  by, 1, 15
NPL. See Nonperforming loans
Nuclear Security Summit, Obama-Xi
  cooperative 2016 discussions at, 15

Obama, Pres. Barack, summits with Xi
  Jinping, 15
Occupational safety, agency failure to
  protect workers, 8, 51–52
OECD. See Organisation for Economic
  Co-operation and Development
One-child policy, labor cost increase and,
  4, 29
Operation Foxhunt, as Chinese political
  security investigations abroad, 23
Organisation for Economic Co-operation
  and Development (OECD), air
  pollution study by, 70

Pacific Rim nations
  U.S. naval exercises with, 18
  See also Asian-Pacific nations
Pakistan, relations with, 16, 21–22
Pensions
  insurance for, 64, 65
  state, vs. personal savings, 63–64
People's Liberation Army (PLA),
  military role of, 17, 18
People's Republic of China. See China
Persian Gulf, strategic communication
  lines with, 16
Philippines, The, U.S. relations with,
  23, 72
PLA. See People's Liberation Army
Plenum Resolution, Sixth (2006)
  possible failure of, 45–46
  16th Central Committee of CPC and,
    discussions of harmonious society,
    45, 55, 71, 95
Plenum Resolution, Third (2013)
  failed initiatives after, 34–41
  government reforms by Xi Jinping in,
    4, 27, 33
  possible failure of, 6, 27, 33–34
Poland, rise of Solidarity economy in, 58
Politics, 23
  viability in, linked to economic
    sustainability, 47, 74, 75n5
  See also Domestic politics
Population, 30f
  displacement of, and dams
    construction, 68, 77n31
  rural, and migration for social
    mobility, 109–111, 111f
  worsening of provincial, and
    environmental problems, 45, 66, 70
Poverty, 54, 107
  income inequality and, in social
    stability, 52–56
  rates of, rural collectives, 52–53, 53f
Power supply failures
  environmental collapse with, 46, 47,
    56–57, 65–71
  trade barriers and, 46, 47, 56–57,
    58–61

Power transition theory, strategic trust and, 21–22
Private sector, 32
  distrust and suppression of, 13, 44
  evolution of, *vs.* state sector, 8–9, 59, 62–64, 76*n*17, 83–85, 102
  SOBs and, 7, 8, 50, 73
Productivity, 60, 103
  gaps in, compared between private- and state-sector firms, 9, 98
  impact of reducing migration and trade costs on, 12–13, 123, 134, 135*t*
  nonagricultural TFP and miscalculations, 100–102
Profits, 13, 91–92, 102–103
Public policy, 70
  debt restructuring as, 34, 35
  government budgeting and fiscal management as, 47–50, 62, 64–65, 73
  infrastructure investment as, 28, 67–68, 69
  privatization absent from, *vs.* discernment from historical record, 84, 87–89, 103–104*n*5
  unsustainable, of increased credit and debt, 41, 46
  See also Government reforms

Regulations, 19, 36, 73
  absence or failure of, in China, 51–52, 65, 75*n*11, 75*nn*8–7
Renminbi (RMB), 35, 86
Rim of the Pacific (RIMPAC) exercise, multinational cooperation in, 18
Rural collectives
  compulsory, and farmers' exit rights, 12, 108, 115, 116–119
  local governments as, with rural land ownership, 11, 107
  poverty rates in, 52–53, 53*f*
  savings rates in, 63–64, 76*n*22
  social structure of, 107–108, 112
  underutilized labor in, 28, 65, 110, 120
Russia, 16, 76*n*16

Salaries
  SOBs and, 50
  SOEs and, 6, 37–38, 40
Samuelson, Paul, on free trade, 72
Sandstorms, 70, 76*n*29
  consequences of, 67, 69
SASAC. *See* State Asset Supervision and Administration Commission
Savings
  excess, as problem, 8, 62
  household, 74*n*1, 103
  rates of, 63, 64, 76*nn*22–23
SCE. *See* State-controlled enterprise sector
Security interests
  key Chinese, extend beyond East Asia, 2, 16–18
  nontraditional, and Chinese cooperation, 3, 24
  respect for differing, 3, 21
Service sector, 102, 116
Shanghai Stock Exchange Index, 6, 36, 37
Shanxi Province
  forced labor in, 51–52, 75*n*11
  water shortage in, 76*n*25
SIC nations. *See specific components, i.e.,* Soviet bloc; China; India
Singapore, 23, 38, 72
Slavery
  forced labor as, 51–52, 75*n*11
  rural, and agency failure, 8, 75*nn*10–11
SOBs. *See* State-owned banks
Social burdens, SOSC conversions and, 94–95, 98, 99*f*
Social media, Weibo as, 37
Social mobility, 109–111, 111–112, 121*n*3
Social safety nets, 58, 59*t*
  U.S. inadequacies in, 58, 61
Social stability, 18
  maintaining, as key security interest, 2, 16, 22
  poverty and income inequality in, 52–56, 75*nn*13–14
  state sector and, goals, 45–46, 71, 98

SOE Reform LSG, 6, 38–39
Soeharto, President, political viability of, 47, 75*n*5
SOEs. *See* State-owned enterprises
Soil erosion, sandstorms and, 67, 76*n*29
SOSC. *See* State-controlled firms
South China Sea, China's expansion and tension in, 1, 3, 15, 21
South Korea, 1
    GDP of, compared to China, 13, 108–109
    income inequality in, 10, 55*t*
    as U.S. ally, 23, 24, 72
Southeast Asia, ASEAN and Cold War in, 72
Soviet bloc, 75*n*4
    globalization and, 58, 59*t*, 60, 76*n*18
Soviet Union
    economies allied with (*see* Soviet bloc)
    end of, 59, 72, 76*n*16
Space security, 2, 15, 17
Sri Lanka, U.S. policy toward, 22
State Asset Supervision and Administration Commission (SASAC), investment companies proposed by, *vs.* Ministry of Finance, 38–39
State Capital Investment and Operation Companies, versions of, 38–39
State-controlled enterprise (SCE) sector
    savings-investment decisions of, 62–65, 76*nn*21–23
    See also State-controlled firms (SOSC); State-owned banks (SOBs); State-owned enterprises (SOEs)
State-controlled firms (SOSC), 8–9
    China's largest enterprises as, 83–84, 102
    definition of, includes some SOEs, 9, 87, 93*t*
    foreign capital in some, 86, 103*n*2
    organization of, varies, 84–87, 88*f*, 89*t*, 90*ff*, 103*nn*3–4

State-owned banks (SOBs)
    bailouts of, 43, 48
    evolution of, as reform, 7, 73
    low returns on investment from, 8, 35, 74*n*1
    nonperforming loans (NPL) by, 46–47, 50, 63, 64
    salaries of, managers, 38, 50
    solvency of, and debt, 7, 43, 74*n*1, 75*n*7
State-owned enterprises (SOEs), 9, 11, 36, 44, 50
    collaboration with private sector by, 45, 63, 83
    as dysfunctional, 8, 91, 102
    reduced salaries in, 37–38, 40
State-owned enterprises (SOEs) reform, 83–104
    attempts at, 6, 8–9, 34, 37–39, 83–84
    challenges for the future in, 9, 102–103
    enterprise classification in, 85–88, 88*f*, 89*t*, 90*f*, 103–104*n*5
    hypotheses of grasping and releasing in, 89–95, 103
    industrial sector and, 88–91, 90*f*
    ownership restructuring in, 84–85, 103, 103*n*1
    regression results, 89*t*, 95–98, 97*t*, 99*t*, 104*n*6
    state restructuring and economic performance in, 98–102
Stock markets, reform of, 5–6, 34, 36–37, 40
Strategic and Economic Dialogue, U.S.-China on long list of cooperative projects, 18
Strategic trust, building for U.S.-Chinese security, 2, 15, 21–23
Subsidies, rigged currency and, 57
Suharto. *See* Soeharto
Summits, dialogues, and meetings, U.S.-China and emerging security interests, 15, 17, 18
Supply-Side Structural Reform, as new imitative after failure of Xi's economic reforms, 40–41

TAA. *See* Trade Adjustment Assistance
Taiwan, 63
    economic growth rate in, compared to
        China, 28, 31–32
    foreign capital from, in some SOSC,
        86, 103*n*2
    GDP of, compared to China, 13,
        108–109
    income inequality in, compared to
        China, 10, 55*t*
    labor costs change in, and economic
        growth, 4, 29
    as U.S. nonally partner, 23, 72
Technological growth
    restrictions on technology sales affect,
        3, 17
    sustained economic and, among key
        security interests, 2, 16, 21
    wages and, in ICT revolution, 60, 61,
        76*n*19
Temasek, as Singapore's sovereign
    wealth funds, 38
TFP (Total factor productivity), 100–102
Thailand, U.S. relations with, 22, 72
Three Gorges Dam, 68
Tibetan population, social discontent in,
    16, 23
Trade, 1, 16, 20, 83
    exports during high-growth era, 28,
        51
    GATT-WTO free, negotiations, 71–72
    GDP growth rate and, 45, 134, 135*tt*
    internal and international costs of,
        12–13, 123, 126–132, 131*t*, 132*t*,
        136, 137
    new Silk Road for, 16–17
    noncompliance with international,
        sanctions, 19–20
    regional, shares in China, 127, 128*t*,
        137
    U.S.-China, deficits, 57, 59*t*, 61
Trade Adjustment Assistance (TAA)
    program, skill upgrades for
    younger workers, 61
Trade unions, decline of, 61

Trade wars
    as export collapse causing social
        unrest, 8, 46
    possible, and conflicts between China,
        EU, and U.S., 56–57, 61
Trans-Pacific Partnership, power
    transition theory and, 21–22
Twitter (social media), as Weibo in
    China, 37

Uighur population. *See* Uyghur
    population
Underemployment, rural collectives and,
    28, 65
Unemployment, 64, 74*n*1
    export of, from China, 57–58, 59*t*
    initial, benefits compared
        internationally, 58–59
United Kingdom, 55*t*, 58, 59*t*
United States (U.S.), 18, 123
    defects in the, economy, 57–61, 65
    GDP of, 44, 57, 59*t*, 75*n*4
    income inequality in, 54, 55*t*
    mobilizing allies and partners of, 2, 3,
        15, 23–24
    public attention to newly changed
        China in, 2, 3, 15, 24
    relationships with China and, 1–3, 13,
        18, 21, 24, 56–57, 70
    trade and migration in, compared,
        134–136, 135*t*
U.S. Congress, trade considerations of,
    43, 57, 61
U.S. Department of Homeland Security,
    18
U.S. Department of Labor, 61
U.S. Department of State, China's power
    status and, 1, 15, 16–18
U.S. Office of Personnel Management,
    data theft from, 17
Urban areas, 44
    agglomeration effect in, 110–111
    exclusivity of, and hukou system, 10,
        107, 111–112, 121*n*2
    land categories in, 11, 116, 117–118

Urban areas, *cont.*
  migration to, for social mobility by
    rural population, 109–111, 111*f,*
    120
  nonagricultural trade costs for, 130,
    131*t*
  savings rates in, 63–64
Urban planning, 107
  See also under China, central
    planning in
Uyghur population, social discontent in,
  16, 18, 23

Vietnam, 23
  China expansion and conflict with,
    14, 28
Voluntarism, 114–115, 117

Wages
  globalization and, 60, 76*nn*18–19
  insurance for, as safety net, 61, 65
  low Chinese, and U.S. competition,
    57–58, 59*t,* 76*n*15
  migrant worker, over time, 29*f,* 65,
    107
  unskilled Chinese, and offshoring
    production, 4, 28
Water pollution, 76*n*27, 77*n*30
  economic development and, 65, 68
Water shortages, 66–71, 76*n*25
  aquifers and, 66, 76*n*26
  dams and rivers in, 66, 68
  resource wastage and, 69
Wealth, 13, 37, 38, 83
  barriers to rural accumulation of,
    10–11
  rough road to, in China, 44–57, 65
Weibo, Chinese Twitter known as, 37
Welfare
  aggregate, and impact of reducing
    migration and trade costs, 12–13,
    123, 132, 132*t,* 133–136
  developed countries and, 58, 72
Wen Jiabao
  as former premier of State Council,
    33, 56

Hu-Wen leadership, 45–46, 56
Werner Sichel Lecture Series 2015–2016,
  1
Western Michigan University.
  Department of Economics, as
    lecture series sponsor, 25*n*1
Workers, 28
  compromised safety of, as dereliction
    of government agency duty, 8, 16,
    51–52
  distribution of, and globalization, 10,
    58–59, 59*t,* 72
  layoffs and unrest of, 83, 84
  misallocation of, 100, 102, 123
  older male U.S., and job tenure, 58,
    59*t*
  younger, 29–30, 30*f,* 61
  (*see also* Migrant workers)
World Bank, 1
  pollution survey by, 70, 76*n*24
World Trade Organization (WTO), 64
  China's entry into, 12–13, 28, 43, 123
  free trade regime of, 71, 123
WTO. *See* World Trade Organization

Xi Jinping
  domestic politics of, and effects on
    foreign policy, 3–4
  government intervention approach of,
    4, 5–6, 22, 27, 32–33, 38
  leadership of, 3, 13, 15, 22, 27, 32
  political influence of, on stock
    markets, 5, 6, 37
  SASAC and, 38–39
Xi Jinping economic reform model,
    27–41
  annus horrible of, 34–39
  conclusion and evaluation of, 34–39
  end of miracle growth, 27–31
  policy objectives of, 31–34
  restructuring local government debt,
    34–35
  SOE reform in, 37–39
  stock market reform in, 36–37

Yangtze River, flooding of, 68, 77*n*30

Yellow River, feeders, use, and drying
    of, 66, 68

Zhao Ziyang, as former premier, 33
Zheng Xiaoyu, bribery conviction of, 51
Zhu Rongji, as former premier, 33, 44,
    126

About the Institute

The W.E. Upjohn Institute for Employment Research is a nonprofit research organization devoted to finding and promoting solutions to employment-related problems at the national, state, and local levels. It is an activity of the W.E. Upjohn Unemployment Trustee Corporation, which was established in 1932 to administer a fund set aside by Dr. W.E. Upjohn, founder of The Upjohn Company, to seek ways to counteract the loss of employment income during economic downturns.

The Institute is funded largely by income from the W.E. Upjohn Unemployment Trust, supplemented by outside grants, contracts, and sales of publications. Activities of the Institute comprise the following elements: 1) a research program conducted by a resident staff of professional social scientists; 2) a competitive grant program, which expands and complements the internal research program by providing financial support to researchers outside the Institute; 3) a publications program, which provides the major vehicle for disseminating the research of staff and grantees, as well as other selected works in the field; and 4) an Employment Management Services division, which manages most of the publicly funded employment and training programs in the local area.

The broad objectives of the Institute's research, grant, and publication programs are to 1) promote scholarship and experimentation on issues of public and private employment and unemployment policy, and 2) make knowledge and scholarship relevant and useful to policymakers in their pursuit of solutions to employment and unemployment problems.

Current areas of concentration for these programs include causes, consequences, and measures to alleviate unemployment; social insurance and income maintenance programs; compensation; workforce quality; work arrangements; family labor issues; labor-management relations; and regional economic development and local labor markets.